New Vanguard • 130

US Navy Aircraft Carriers 1942–45

WWII-built ships

Mark Stille • Illustrated by Tony Bryan

First published in Great Britain in 2007 by Osprey Publishing,
Midland House, West Way, Botley, Oxford OX2 0PH, UK
443 Park Avenue South, New York, NY 10016, USA
E-mail: info@ospreypublishing.com

A CIP catalog record for this book is available from the British Library

ISBN: 978 1 84603 037 6

Page layout by: Melissa Orrom Swan, Oxford
Index by Peter Rea
Typeset in Helvetica Neue and ITC New Baskerville
Originated by PPS Grasmere Ltd, Leeds, UK
Printed in China through Worldprint Ltd.

07 08 09 10 11   10 9 8 7 6 5 4 3 2 1

For a catalog of all books published by Osprey Military and Aviation
please contact:

NORTH AMERICA
Osprey Direct, c/o Random House Distribution Center, 400 Hahn Road,
Westminster, MD 21157
E-mail: info@ospreydirect.com

ALL OTHER REGIONS
Osprey Direct UK, P.O. Box 140 Wellingborough, Northants, NN8 2FA, UK
E-mail: info@ospreydirect.co.uk

www.ospreypublishing.com

Editor's note

All photographs in this book are used by the kind permission of the US Naval
Historical Center.

US NAVY AIRCRAFT CARRIERS 1942–45 WWII-BUILT SHIPS

ORIGINS

The US Navy's seven prewar carriers had halted the Japanese advance in the Pacific by the middle of 1942 (see New Vanguard 114, *US Navy Aircraft Carriers 1922–45 Prewar Classes*). This book focuses on the *Essex* class fleet and *Independence* class light carriers that entered US Navy service during the war. These ships would be essential elements in the US Navy's campaign to defeat the Japanese Empire. For the *Essex* class, of the 24 built, 14 saw action during the war. The ships completed after the war and the extensive postwar service and modernization of the *Essex* class are not covered. Of the light carriers, all nine *Independence* class ships saw action. Two other light carriers of the *Saipan* class did not see service during the war and are not discussed.

US Navy mid to late war carrier doctrine

The arrival of a growing number of *Essex* and *Independence* class carriers forced the US Navy to revise its carrier doctrine. Experience from 1942 clearly showed the benefits of operating several carriers together. The early war practice of operating only one or two carriers in a task group was abandoned. Now the arrival of new ships permitted up to four separate carrier task groups to be formed under the Commander, Fast Carrier Force Pacific. Each would operate up to five carriers (usually four) – a mix of fleet and light carriers. These would be typically escorted by a division of battleships, four cruisers (including some dedicated antiaircraft cruisers), and a dozen or so destroyers. To provide the best protection against air attack, the carriers would be placed in the middle of a 4-mile (6.4km) radius circle of escorts. Task groups usually steamed in formation with 12 miles (19.3km) between their centers, leaving

A study in sea power: Task Group 38.3 enters Ulithi Atoll on December 12, 1944, following operations off the Philippines. The lead carrier is *Langley*; she is followed by *Ticonderoga*, three battleships, and four light cruisers. Ulithi Atoll was seized in September 1944 and was used as the fast carriers' primary support anchorage for the remainder of the war.

8 miles (12.9km) from screen to screen. This cruising disposition was based on the effective range of the formation's heavy antiaircraft guns. In addition to presenting any attacker with a continuous wall of antiaircraft fire, it provided enough room for maneuver. It also provided overlapping radar coverage, serving to fill in blind spots.

By 1943, the US Navy had transformed naval warfare in the Pacific. Not only did the numbers of carriers in service dramatically increase, but so did the effectiveness of each ship and its air group. A new generation of aircraft manned by well-trained pilots, improvements in air search and fire control radars, the effectiveness of the Combat Information Center concept that fuzed information on a real-time basis, and the growing number and effectiveness of shipboard antiaircraft guns combined to make US fast carrier task forces essentially immune to conventional air attack. This defensive capability forced the Japanese to rely on night attacks and eventually on kamikaze, or suicide, aircraft.

Together with these technological advances, there was a corresponding operational leap. A sophisticated mobile logistics capability was developed which allowed the US Navy to forward deploy to fleet anchorages and operate the Fast Carrier Force at sea for months at a time using underway replenishment. This maintained a high operational tempo, keeping the Japanese off-balance, and provided the capability not just to raid, as the Imperial Japanese Navy's carrier task force had done early in the war, but to project power on a sustained basis. It was a war-winning formula.

DEVELOPMENT

Mid to late war air groups and aircraft

In 1942, carrier air groups were assigned numbers with the first being Air Group 9. In June 1944, the designation of air groups was changed to reflect the type of carrier they were assigned to. An *Essex* class carrier's air group was designated CVG and an *Independence* class carrier's group was designated CVLG.

The ability of the US Navy to sustain operations at sea was one of the unheralded reasons for the American victory in the Pacific. Here *Hornet* is shown refueling from an oiler in August 1944. As an example of the US Navy's logistical capabilities, between October 6, 1944 and January 26, 1945, the Fast Carrier Force was at sea for 13 of 16 weeks. To maintain this effort required a dedicated force of 34 fleet oilers.

COMPOSITION OF *ESSEX* CLASS AIR GROUPS

	Fighters	Dive bombers	Torpedo bombers
1943	36	36	18
July 1944	54 (4 night)	24	18
December 1944	73 (4 night)	15	15

Essex in May 1943 during work-ups. This view shows her early air group that included SBD Dauntless dive bombers (the aircraft on the aft portion of the flight deck without folding wings), TBF Avenger torpedo bombers, and F6F Hellcat fighters. Early *Essex* class air groups were notable for their large proportion of strike aircraft at the expense of fighters. *Essex* appears in her early configuration with five radio masts, a single stern 40mm quadruple mount, and no starboard outboard sponsons. Interestingly, she would remain basically unaltered throughout the war.

Essex class carriers, as commissioned, had an air group with a large fighter squadron of 36 fighters, plus 18 aircraft scout, dive bomber, and torpedo squadrons. One additional dive bomber for liaison duties was included for a total air group of 91 aircraft. There were also nine reserve aircraft, three of each type.

By 1944, the need for a dedicated scout bomber squadron was gone, so the two squadrons equipped with dive bombers were combined into a single 24-aircraft squadron. The fighter squadron grew and included special radar-equipped night fighter and photo-reconnaissance fighter variants. As the kamikaze threat became paramount, the number of fighter aircraft was again increased in December 1944. Now a single 73-aircraft fighter squadron was embarked and the number of strike aircraft reduced to 30, organized into two 15-aircraft dive bomber and torpedo squadrons. With 73 aircraft and 110 pilots, the fighter squadron had become too unwieldy. In January 1945 it was split into two squadrons, one with

36 fighters, the other with 36 fighter-bombers. In practice, the two squadrons were interchangeable. In 1945, two air groups discarded their dive bomber squadron and operated 93 fighters and 15 torpedo aircraft.

Most *Essex* class carriers took a number of different air groups into action. With a large pool of aviators available, the US Navy could rotate tired veteran air groups. In addition to casualties, the air groups had to contend with fatigue brought on by incessant combat. In January 1944, it was decided that complete air groups would be rotated after six to nine months of combat. This was later shortened in April to six months as the pace of the war intensified. It became necessary to rotate some air groups after only four months. This contributed to the requirement to bring US Marine Corps fighter squadrons aboard the fleet carriers in late 1944. Eventually, two air groups were planned for each carrier.

The arrival of the new carriers coincided with the arrival of new aircraft. Most prominent among these was the Grumman F6F Hellcat. The first mass-produced variant, the F6F-3, entered service in 1943 and was faster and better armored and had more firepower than its Japanese counterparts. The Hellcat was the mainstay fighter of the US Navy from 1943 to 1945, with over 12,000 built. The improved F6F-5 began to enter service in April 1944. Late in the war, some CVGs received the Vought F4U Corsair. Introduced in 1943, the Corsair would remain land-based until late 1944, when the kamikaze crisis and a fighter shortage brought it aboard fleet carriers on a permanent basis. With its speed and ruggedness, it proved to be the best carrier fighter of the war.

Into the mid-war period, the dive bomber role continued to be filled by the Douglas SBD Dauntless. The upgraded Dauntless SBD-5 was not finally replaced until July 1944. Its replacement was the Curtiss SB2C Helldiver. This aircraft experienced a long gestation period before being wholly accepted for fleet use. Difficult to handle, it possessed no greater range than the Dauntless, carried a similar bomb load, and proved more difficult to maintain. It was, however, faster and more rugged. The torpedo bomber mission was handled by the Grumman TBF Avenger from mid-1942 to the end of the war. This aircraft also performed in a level bomber role. Some 7,500 were built under the TBF and the General Motors TBM designation.

Hellcat fighters preparing to take off from *Ticonderoga*. The two leading aircraft are F6F-5N variants; the pod on the wing contains a radar for night operations.

Weapons

The war-built US carriers were well provided for in terms of antiaircraft protection. For long-range air defense, the mainstay weapon was the 5in/38 dual-purpose gun. This weapon had been fitted on the prewar *Yorktown* class and had proved itself to be an excellent gun possessing good accuracy, a long barrel life, and, most importantly, a high rate of fire. It was the finest weapon of its type in service during the war and remained in service long after. Aside from making a brief appearance on the lead ship, the *Independence* class did not carry the 5in/38 gun. In the middle of the war the effectiveness of the 5in was further increased when the VT (variable timed) fuze, containing a tiny radio transmitter in the nose of the shell, entered service. The fuze sensed the reflected radiation off the target and detonated the shell within 30ft (approx 9m) – a lethal range. When used with radar fire direction, it was a deadly combination.

Long-range antiaircraft protection for *Essex* class carriers was provided by the redoubtable 5in/38 dual-purpose gun. Two twin mounts were located forward and aft of the island; the forward mounts on *Intrepid* are shown here, trained to starboard. This photograph of *Intrepid* was taken after June 1944, as the ship has received the modified bridge and the SC-2 radar has been moved to the starboard side of the stack.

SPECIFICATIONS FOR THE 5IN/38 GUN

Bore	5in (127mm)
Shell weight	55lb (25kg)
Muzzle velocity	2,600ft/sec (792.4m/sec)
Maximum range	18,200yd (16,642m)
Rate of fire	15–20 rounds/min

The Mark 37 Director provided primary fire control for the 5in/38. On *Essex* class ships two were fitted on the island, one forward and one aft. This director was provided with a twin parabolic trough antenna Mark 4 Radar to further increase its performance. The Mark 37 proved very successful in handling all but the fastest targets. Later, the Mark 4 was replaced by the Mark 12 Radar, which used the same antenna, but which offered a limited blind-fire capability. Introduced with the Mark 12 was the Mark 22 Height-finder Radar. This was a small parabolic antenna attached to one side of the Mark 12. When completed, early *Essex* class ships received the Mark 4 Radar, with later ships receiving the Mark 12/22. Earlier ships got the Mark 12/22 upgrade during the course of refit or repair.

The next layer of air defense was provided by the 40mm Bofors gun. These entered service on *Essex* class ships in quadruple mounts and on *Independence* class ships in quadruple and double mounts. These proved very effective in service, but later in the war even these lacked the power to stop onrushing kamikazes. Fire control for the 40mm Bofors was usually provided by the Mark 51 Director. This was a simple and lightweight system and incorporated the Mark 14 Gunsight. It proved very effective out to about 3,000yd (2,743m). Early ships used a mix of the simple Mark 51 and the

Shown here is a 40mm quadruple mount on *Hornet* in February 1945, during the raids on Tokyo. This is the gun mount on the port side of the flight deck, just forward of the aft pair of 5in/38 single guns. Note the expended shells to the right of the photo and the ready rounds lining the gun tub. The 40mm gun was probably the most successful medium-range antiaircraft gun of the war.

more complex Mark 49 Director that was coupled with the Mark 19 Radar in an attempt to provide a blind-fire capability. The Mark 49 proved unsuccessful in service and was quickly removed. Beginning in late 1944, some Mark 51s were replaced by the similar Mark 57 with the Mark 29 Radar. The Mark 57 did provide a blind-fire capability. In 1945, the Mark 63 was introduced, which placed its associated radar directly on the 40mm mount. In some cases, both the Mark 51 and Mark 57 Directors could be used to direct 5in guns, thus increasing the number of targets that could be engaged by the ship's 5in battery.

SPECIFICATIONS FOR THE 40MM BOFORS GUN

Bore	1.575in (40mm)
Shell weight	1.985lb (.9kg)
Muzzle velocity	2,890ft/sec (880.8m/sec)
Maximum range	11,000yd (10,058m)
Rate of fire	160 rounds/min (less in service)

The standard short-range antiaircraft weapon aboard US carriers after 1942 was the Swiss-designed 20mm Oerlikon gun. It was originally fitted in a single mount, but a double mount was later introduced to increase the weapon's firepower. The 20mm gun was air-cooled, required no external power source, and was lightweight, so it was fitted in large numbers. It was a last-ditch weapon that, by war's end, had fallen out of favor, as its weight of shell was clearly inadequate to stop kamikazes. The 20mm was equipped with a ring sight for aiming, and fire was spotted by the use of tracers. The Mark 14 Gunsight could be mounted on the 20mm to provide target tracking. On both *Essex* and *Independence* class ships, these guns were usually fitted on platforms along the flight deck.

Each *Essex* class carrier mounted a large number of single 20mm guns. Most were fitted on platforms alongside the flight deck. The 20mm gun was a reliable weapon that required no external power source and could be bolted to the deck anywhere with a clear field of fire. These are aboard *Hornet* in February 1945; by this time the weapon was no longer in favor as it lacked the stopping power to break up incoming kamikazes before they hit the ship.

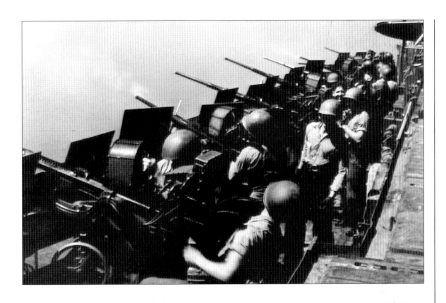

SPECIFICATIONS FOR THE 20MM OERLIKON GUN

Bore	.7874in (20mm)
Shell weight	.271lb (.122kg)
Muzzle velocity	2,740ft/sec (835.1m/sec)
Maximum range	4,800yd (4,389m)
Rate of fire	450 rounds/min (less in service)

Radar

The use and development of radar proved to be a critical aspect of carrier operations in the war's early period. Eventually, it became a central component to US carrier doctrine. Radar proved essential to solving the problem of fleet air defense. Only it could provide the warning needed to direct fighters to incoming threats. Radar information was fed into a Combat Information Center (CIC) and in turn used by the adjacent Fighter Direction Office. In early ships, a crowded CIC was placed in the island. Later in the war, when these ships received a bridge modification that expanded the size of the flag plot, the CIC was moved to the gallery deck (the level below the flight deck). Some ships, particularly those built late in the war, had the CIC moved deep into the ship below the main armored deck. This offered much better protection than the vulnerable gallery deck location right under the unarmored flight deck.

No provision was made in the original *Essex* design for radar. Several were added, but the cramped placement of antennae on the island caused mutual interference problems that were never really solved. Additionally, placement on the island made for smoke damage from the stack and crowded conditions in the radar room. Throughout the war there were a number of different radar fits, but originally it was envisioned to give the *Essex* class carriers a primary air search radar, a back-up air search radar, and two surface search radar. With the addition of Identification Friend or Foe (IFF) equipment, radar beacons, the YE aircraft homing beacon (a radio transmitter with a 30-mile range, sending a specific signal allowing the pilot to approximate the carrier's bearing), and later passive and active electronic countermeasure gear, this made for a growing profusion of antennae.

The original long-range air search radar was the SK placed on the radar platform just forward of the stack. The SK had a 17ft^2 (5.1m^2) bed spring antenna with a range of 100 nautical miles (185km) against targets at an altitude of 10,000ft (3,050m). Later, the SK-2 was introduced – this was an improved SK with a dish antenna. The back-up air search radar, the SC-2, was originally placed on a platform on the side of the stack. The SC-2 had a 15ft by 4ft 6in (4.5m by 1.4m) antenna and a range of 80 nautical miles (148km) against targets at 10,000ft (3,050m). Late in the war, the SR replaced the SC series. Its primary improvement was providing shock mounting. The SR had a 15ft by 6ft (4.5m by 1.8m) antenna and a range of 110 nautical miles (204km). Also on the radar platform (usually on the topmast) was an SG for surface search. The second SG set was usually mounted on the rear of the stack to cover the blind spot to the rear of the ship.

This is the radar-plotting screen aboard *Hornet* on August 5, 1944, while the carrier was operating off the Bonin Islands. Several of the Bonins are noted on the left of the display and Japanese air activity (Raid I) is noted to the northeast of the ship. The incorporation of radar into carrier doctrine was essential in providing the carrier task force with a high degree of protection from conventional Japanese air attacks.

With broad beam air search radars, it was still a problem to determine the height of incoming aircraft. This information was essential for effective fighter direction. Accordingly, the SM height-finder was introduced for fighter control. It used a narrow beam to pinpoint contacts gained by air search radars. It had a 6ft (1.8m) dish antenna, a range of 50 nautical miles (93km) out to 10,000ft (3,050m), and an elevation accuracy of 500ft (152.4m). An SM height-finder radar prototype was mounted on *Lexington* in March 1943; this radar proved successful in service and production sets were fitted on other carriers in 1943. When introduced, height-finder radars occupied the best position on the forward portion of the radar platform. On most ships, the platform was lengthened to fit both air search and height-finder radars. The lightweight successor to the SM, the SP, was introduced in 1945. It possessed an 8ft (2.4m) diameter dish antenna with a maximum range of 80 nautical miles (148km).

CHRONOLOGY

The following is an overview of the US Navy's Pacific offensive from its tentative start in 1943 to final victory in 1945. Because this offensive was made possible by the introduction of the *Essex* and *Independence* class carriers, this chronology is useful to gauge the steady increase in the numbers of carriers in service, as well as the increasing tempo of activity and the major operations.

1943
August *Yorktown, Essex*, and *Independence* conduct a raid against
   Marcus Island in the Central Pacific.
September *Lexington, Princeton*, and *Belleau Wood* raid Tarawa
   in the Gilbert Islands.
October *Essex, Yorktown, Lexington, Independence, Belleau Wood*,
   and *Cowpens* raid Wake Island.
November *Princeton* and the older fleet carrier *Saratoga* strike
   the Japanese base at Rabaul. Joined later by *Essex, Bunker Hill*,

and *Independence* for additional strikes. Severe losses are inflicted on land-based Japanese naval air units.

November Operation *Galvanic*: invasion of the Gilbert Islands. Now the Fast Carrier Force has expanded to four separate task groups including fleet carriers *Essex, Yorktown, Bunker Hill,* and *Lexington,* and light carriers *Independence, Cowpens, Belleau Wood, Monterey,* and *Princeton.* These are joined by prewar fleet carriers *Saratoga* and *Enterprise.* During the operation *Independence* is torpedoed by aircraft in a dusk attack.

December Raid on Kwajalein in the Marshall Islands by *Essex, Yorktown, Lexington, Bunker Hill, Belleau Wood,* and *Monterey. Lexington* is torpedoed by aircraft in a night attack.

1944

January Task Force 58 formed under command of Rear Admiral Marc Mitscher.

January Operation *Flintlock*: invasion of the Marshalls. Kwajalein is seized. Four *Essex* class, two prewar carriers, and six *Independence* class carriers operate in four task groups. *Intrepid, Cabot,* and *Langley* join the fray.

February First raid on the important Central Pacific naval base at Truk by *Enterprise,* four *Essex,* and four *Independence* class carriers. Truk is neutralized and 250 Japanese aircraft and 39 warships and merchants are destroyed. *Intrepid* is torpedoed in a night air attack.

Franklin under attack off the coast of Japan on March 19, 1945. The ship is in its late war configuration with the modified bridge and three visible starboard side 40mm sponsons. The large circular SK-2 radar is fitted outboard of the stack and the SC-2 radar is just visible on the rear of the radar platform. The ship is listing to starboard – not because of battle damage, but owing to the large amounts of water being used to fight the fires on board.

This independent strike by nine carriers is the largest of the war to date; it confirms US carrier doctrine and proves the Fast Carrier Force to be the most powerful naval force in the world.

February Strikes against the Mariana Islands with three *Essex* and three *Independence* class carriers. The Truk and Marianas raids confirm the strategic capabilities of the Fast Carrier Force when permitted to exercise operational freedom. They also demonstrate the futility of Japan's island chain defense strategy as the US Navy simply deploys overwhelming numbers against any part of the chain – once neutralized, non-essential islands can be bypassed.

March Now part of the 5th Fleet, Task Force 58 neutralizes the Japanese naval base at Palau with four *Essex* and six *Independence* class carriers. *Hornet* joins the force.

April Fast carriers support General MacArthur's landings at Hollandia in New Guinea. *Bataan* joins Task Force 58.

April Task Force 58 returns to pound Truk.

June Operation *Forager*: invasion of the Marianas. The Imperial Navy commits its carrier force for the first time since October 1942. With nine Japanese carriers facing 15 US Navy carriers (including *Enterprise, Hornet, Yorktown, Bunker Hill, Wasp, Lexington, Essex*, and eight of the nine *Independence* class carriers), this is the largest carrier battle in history. On June 19, 450 defending Hellcats and antiaircraft fire destroy 300 Japanese aircraft for a loss of only 29 Hellcats. No US carriers are sunk and only two are slightly damaged, but the Japanese lose almost their entire carrier-based air force and three carriers. The battle of the Philippine Sea marks the effective end of the Japanese carrier force.

August Task Force 38 is formed under the Third Fleet. This dual command system keeps the same ships, but changes their fleet and task force designations. This allows the alternate command staff to plan future operations.

September Strikes against Palau and the southern Philippines in preparation for the invasion of the Philippines. Addition of *Franklin* gives Task Force 38 eight fleet carriers (seven *Essex* class) and eight *Independence* class.

October Strikes against Formosa (Taiwan). Over 500 Japanese aircraft are destroyed; no carriers are hit. Addition of *Hancock* gives Task Force 38 17 carriers embarking over 1,000 aircraft.

October Invasion of Leyte and the battle of Leyte Gulf. The Imperial Japanese Navy commits its remaining strength to stop the US from seizing the Philippines and cutting Japan's access to resources in the

Princeton soon after being bombed on the morning of October 24, 1944. This picture shows the ship on fire, with smoke columns resulting from a series of explosions from aircraft in the hangar. Later in the day the ship's torpedo store blew up and the ship was finally scuttled. *Princeton* was the only *Independence* class carrier lost during the war.

OPPOSITE **This photograph, taken at Ulithi Atoll on December 8, 1944, epitomizes the striking power of the *Essex* class in the US Navy's Pacific War campaign. Pictured in the front row are *Wasp, Yorktown, Hornet, Hancock*, and *Ticonderoga*, all in various "dazzle" schemes. Behind them is *Lexington*, easily discernible in her solid Measure 21 scheme, and two *Independence* class light carriers.**

Dutch East Indies. Task Force 38 sinks four Japanese carriers and superbattleship *Musashi*. This marks the end of the Imperial Navy as an effective fighting force. Light carrier *Princeton* is lost to air attack.

October Advent of the kamikaze. Several *Essex* and *Independence* class carriers are hit by suicide aircraft. Most often, damage is light and the ships can quickly return to service. However, a mounting number of ships are forced to leave the combat zone for repair. Kamikazes will be the sternest test for the fast carriers. In response, more fighters are added to air groups at the expense of bombers. Marine Corps fighter squadrons are added to air groups to make up for fighter shortages.

November–December Task Force 38 continues to provide air cover to the Leyte landings under constant kamikaze attack. By November, losses to kamikazes have reduced Task Force 38 to three task groups with seven *Essex* and five *Independence* class carriers.

On October 30, 1944, kamikazes attacked the Fast Carrier Force while it was operating in support of the landings on Leyte in the Philippines. Viewed from an escorting destroyer, this is the result; on the left is *Belleau Wood* and on the right is *Franklin*. The kamikaze threat would grow increasingly severe for the remainder of the war, but not a single light or fleet carrier was lost to kamikaze damage.

1945

January Task Force 38 rampages into the South China Sea to devastate Japanese shipping. The Philippine campaign finally ends; from September to the end of January, the fast carriers put on a remarkable display of endurance, covering a series of landings while crippling the Japanese fleet and destroying thousands of aircraft.

January Task Force 58 takes command of the Fast Carrier Force.

February Invasion of Iwo Jima. *Bennington, Randolph, Shangri-La,* and *Bon Homme Richard* join the Fast Carrier Force. Task Force 58 strikes the Tokyo area; this is the first carrier strike against Japan since April 1942. Task Force 58 deploys five task groups with nine *Essex,* five *Independence,* and a special task group of night carriers with prewar carriers *Enterprise* and *Saratoga.*

March Task Force 58 strikes the southern Japanese home island of Kyushu in preparation for the invasion of Okinawa. Heavy losses are suffered; *Franklin, Wasp,* and *Enterprise* are crippled and forced to leave for repairs.

April–May Task Force 58 provides air cover for the Okinawa landing. Superbattleship *Yamato* is sunk with one light cruiser and four destroyers for a loss of only ten aircraft. For 92 days the fast carriers

maintain a 60 square mile (155 square km) station less than 350 miles (563km) from Kyushu under constant kamikaze attack.

May Task Force 38 takes command of the Fast Carrier Force.

July–August Strikes against Japan are conducted in preparation for the planned landings in Kyushu. For this final push Task Force 38 musters ten *Essex* and six *Independence* class units supported by a Royal Navy task group of four fleet carriers. Air opposition is much reduced as the Japanese hoard their remaining aircraft for the expected invasion.

September Japan surrenders.

THE *ESSEX* CLASS

Origins

The *Essex* class had its roots in the prewar 20,000-ton (18,144-tonne) *Yorktown* class design. Design work for what was to become the *Essex* class began in June 1939. The most important design feature of the new class was the desire to operate a larger air group. At the same time it was recognized that the aircraft being operated would be larger and heavier, requiring more deck space to handle the desired size of air group. This could not be achieved on a *Yorktown* size hull. It was also desired that the new class possess increased protection. Moreover, endurance was an important factor, since the ships were designed for a war in the Pacific against the Japanese. Eventually, what emerged was a design of some 27,100 tons (24,585 tonnes) with an air group of 90 aircraft, a range of 15,000 nautical miles at 15 knots (27,780km at 27.8km/h), and a top design speed of 33 knots (61.1km/h).

The first ship in the class, CV-9, later *Essex*, was ordered as part of the Naval Expansion Act of 1938. However, as events in Europe unfolded, it was obvious that the US Navy would require dramatic expansion. The Two Ocean Navy Act of June 1940 allocated funds for three more carriers. When later that same month France fell, another seven carriers were funded in August 1940. After the attack on Pearl Harbor, another two were funded. A second wave of an additional ten ships was ordered in August 1942 and three more were ordered in June 1943. Of the 26 ships ordered, all but two would be completed. Of the 17 completed before war's end, 14 would arrive in the Pacific in time to see action.

Essex was launched on July 31, 1942, many months ahead of schedule. At 27,500 tons (33,003 tonnes) design standard displacement, she was the largest American carrier built to date, with the exception of the two *Lexington* class carriers that were converted from battlecruisers.

Five shipyards were eventually active in the *Essex* building program. The Newport News shipyard in Virginia and the Bethlehem Quincy shipyard in Massachusetts delivered most of the early ships. Other facilities to complete *Essex* carriers were the Navy Yards at Norfolk, Philadelphia, and New York. Construction on the class went smoothly, aided by the high priority accorded to carrier production. The lead ship was completed in only 17 months – some 15 months early. Construction and design emphasized economical use of materials, both to reduce use of steel and therefore weight, and also to keep construction as easy as possible, thus speeding completion. Where possible, all steel parts were kept straight and flat. The high priority of carriers and the efficiency of American yards meant that an *Essex* class ship could be completed in as little as 14 months, and no more than 22.5 months, with the average being 18.5 months.

Design and construction

There were actually two *Essex* sub-types. Most ships were built to the "short-hull" design with specifications of 872ft (265.8m) length overall. Of the 14 ships to see combat service in the Pacific, four ships were completed to a "long-hull" design with an overall length of 888ft (270.6m). The difference was the clipper bow fitted to the long-hull units; both sub-types had the same waterline length. The clipper bow improved sea keeping and allowed for the provision of two bow-mounted 40mm quadruple mounts.

For the first time on a US carrier, underwater protection was provided by a system with two outboard voids filled with liquids and two inboard voids. In theory, the liquid layers would absorb the shock of a torpedo explosion and the voids would contain any fragments and leakage. This system extended about the same length as the armored belt, protecting the ship's vitals. Protection was designed to be adequate against 500lb (227kg) TNT. The triple bottom system consisted of two layers on the bottom of the hull. The inner bottom ran the whole length of the ship but the third bottom only covered the vitals.

The flight deck was not armored, as the weight penalties for this would have been prohibitive. The main deck (actually the hangar deck) armor of 2½in (6.4cm) was designed to be sufficient to stop penetration by a 1,000lb (454kg) bomb dropped from 10,000ft (3,050m). Another

Essex **class carriers proved very resilient to bomb and kamikaze damage. Here** *Bunker Hill* **burns after suffering two kamikaze hits on May 11, 1945. The crew brought the fires under control and the ship survived.**

1½in (3.8cm) of armor was fitted on the fourth deck. Side armor was sufficient to defeat 6in (15.2cm) shells, which designers believed would be sufficient against cruiser attack. The belt armor had a maximum depth of 4in (10.2cm) tapering to 2½in (6.4cm). The area protected totaled 508ft (154.8m) including the ship's machinery, magazines, and aviation gas storage. Steering gear was protected by 4½in (11.4cm) side armor, with an aft bulkhead of 4in (10.2cm), and was covered by 2½in (6.4cm) and closed on the bottom with ¾in (1.9cm) of armor. There was also a ⅝in (1.6cm) armored platform over the forward and aft magazines.

Propulsion

Propulsive machinery was fitted into six compartments below the fourth deck, with each separated by a watertight bulkhead. The positioning of the engine and boiler rooms was alternated so that a single hit could not destroy all propulsive power. The *Essex* class was the first US carrier to use this concept of two independent groups of machinery. This was an important design upgrade from the previous *Yorktown* class.

The ship's four propellers were driven by four sets of Westinghouse steam turbines driven by steam from eight Babcock and Wilcox oil-fired boilers. All boilers vented through a small stack on the island. This machinery produced 150,000 shaft horse power. With oil bunkerage of between 6,161 and 6,331 tons (5,589 and 5,743 tonnes), the ships possessed enormous range – up to 17,250 nautical miles (31,947km) for the long-hull ships. The entire system proved very efficient in service, providing excellent range and no major maintenance difficulties. This was a result of the US Navy's development of high-power, lightweight machinery that provided weight savings and advantages in fuel consumption.

Armament

The protective antiaircraft armament of the *Essex* class was much increased over the *Yorktown* class. For long-range antiaircraft protection, a total of 12 5in/38 guns were fitted. These came in two different types of mount. Four dual mounts were fitted on the starboard side, two forward and two aft of the island. These were on the flight deck, so presented a slight impediment to flight operations. On the port side, four additional guns were fitted in single mounts. These were placed in pairs on sponsons just below the flight deck to minimize the impact on the size of the flight deck.

The *Essex* class was originally designed to carry eight 40mm quadruple mounts. These were situated one on the bow, one at the stern (offset to port), two on the port side adjacent to the pairs of single 5in guns fore and aft, and four on the island (two forward and two aft). Throughout the war, the number of these very effective weapons was increased. Additions included two mounts on the hangar deck level port side in place of the hangar deck catapult, and an additional mount on the stern. In mid-1943, further additions were

An F6F-3 Hellcat fighter preparing to take off from *Yorktown* in 1943. The two 40mm quadruple mounts located on the front of the island are clearly visible. Later in the war, the lower 40mm mount was removed to permit the expansion of the flag bridge. Between the two 40mm mounts is a smaller tub containing a Mark 51 Fire Control Director.

approved, including two mounts on sponsons on the hangar deck level on the starboard quarter. These were originally fitted in recessed mountings so as not to interfere with a Panama Canal passage, but later they were placed in sponsons to provide a better arc of fire. Three additional mounts were added below the island on detachable sponsons. Finally, two mounts were added on platforms just below the flight deck on the port side. The only decrease in the 40mm fit was the removal of one of the quadruple mounts on the forward part of the island to allow the flag bridge to be expanded. When ships were under refit, some or all of these modifications were added. Short-hull ships could receive all but a second 40mm mount on the bow, making for a possible total of 17 quadruple mounts, with a second quadruple mount on the bow: long-hull ships embarked as many as 18 quadruple mounts. The addition of these extra quadruple mounts posed a great increase in top weight, but was considered essential to enhance the ship's antiaircraft protection. See the individual ships' histories for the precise fit on each ship.

As designed, the *Essex* class mounted 46 20mm guns on platforms just below the flight deck level. This number rose to as many as 58 on some ships by the summer of 1943. By 1945, in response to the kamikaze threat, the dual mount 20mm was introduced, taking the place of some of the single mounts. Also in response to the kamikaze threat, in 1945 *Wasp* and *Lexington* received Army quadruple .50-cal. machine-gun mounts on a trial basis.

Aircraft-handling facilities

The central design feature of the *Essex* class was the ability to quickly handle a large air group. Because the air group was so large, it could not be accommodated in the hangar deck and the US Navy practice of using a continuous deck park was adopted.

Hornet on March 27, 1945, operating off Okinawa. The ship is in a Measure 33/3a scheme. The large deck park is typical of American fleet carriers. The many aircraft still spotted forward suggest that she has just recovered aircraft and is in the process of re-spotting the flight deck for future operations.

The flight deck was 108ft (32.9m) wide and 862ft (262.7m) long. After favorable reports were gained on the performance of the deck edge elevator on the first *Wasp* (CV-7), this change was approved for the *Essex* class. Thus, three large elevators were installed, one centerline forward, one offset to starboard near the island, and the deck edge elevator located on the port side amidships. Elevator cycle time was 45 seconds, including time to load the aircraft on and off the elevator. Weight capacity was 28,000lb (12,700kg) for the centerline elevators and 18,000lb (8,165kg) for the deck edge elevator.

To speed aircraft launch times, one flush deck catapult was mounted forward. This was the 18,000lb (8,165kg) capacity H (hydraulic) Mark IV B. Use of the catapult was not common in the early stages of the war. As long as aircraft were not too heavy to make a rolling take-off, this was the easier and preferred method. However, as aircraft became heavier, use of catapults increased. By war's end, some carriers were making 40 percent of launches by catapult. Doing so also increased flight deck flexibility as it permitted a launch to be made in any wind condition and allowed for a launch of a larger deck load.

An open hangar deck was retained – this allowed aircraft to be warmed up on the hangar deck and then moved to the flight deck, greatly speeding launch times. A series of large roller curtains were used to close the hangar to accommodate tactical requirements or weather conditions. The hangar itself was 654ft by 70ft (199.3m by 21.3m) with 18ft (5.5m) clearance. Six ships received a double-action type catapult mounted athwartships in the forward hangar bay. This attempt to improve tactical flexibility proved impracticable and all were eventually removed.

Another impracticable feature was the inclusion of a full set of arresting gear forward. This would allow the ship to retain its aviation capabilities if bomb damage destroyed the recovery facilities in the rear of the ship. Despite its lack of feasibility, the forward arresting gear was not removed from the ships until 1944.

The amount of aviation gasoline was increased from 178,000 gallons (673,803 liters) in the *Yorktown* class to between 225,000 and 232,000 gallons (851,717 and 878,215 liters) for short-hulled ships and between 209,000 and 242,000 gallons (878,216 and 916,069 liters) for long-hulled ships. The amounts varied as different modifications were incorporated for protection of the gasoline storage system. Later ships had the aviation tanks moved aft to better-protected locations and the tanks were modified to insert seawater into the area of consumed gasoline. The total aviation ordnance that could be stored in two primary magazines totaled 625.5 tons (567.4 tonnes).

Wartime modifications

The *Essex* class proved able to accommodate a large number of wartime modifications. Most of these have already been mentioned and specific details are provided in each ship's operational history. However, the total of these changes made the ships seriously top heavy and therefore less stable. It was estimated that, with the reduction of stability, three or four torpedo hits would have resulted in a high probability of loss. It was fortunate that none of the ships suffered war damage that threatened their stability. *Franklin* suffered extensive topside damage but developed stability problems due to the use of massive amounts of fire-fighting water. The only ships that took torpedo hits, *Lexington* and *Intrepid*, took only a single hit astern and were not threatened with sinking.

Wartime modifications also made for severe overcrowding conditions. On trials, *Essex* had a crew of 226 officers and 2,880 enlisted men, several hundred more than her original design. In 1945, *Intrepid* had a crew of 382 officers and 3,003 enlisted men. This made berthing and messing difficult, and living conditions in tropical areas were particularly uncomfortable.

Operational histories
Essex (CV-9)

Built by Newport News and commissioned on December 31, 1942, *Essex* first saw action during the Marcus Island raid. Later she participated in most of the major engagements of the war, including the first Truk raid, Philippine Sea, and Leyte Gulf. *Essex* was damaged by kamikaze attack on November 25, 1944, but returned for the war's final stages. After the war, she was decommissioned in January 1947, but returned to service in 1951 after modernization. *Essex* fought in the Korean War; she was decommissioned for the final time in 1969 and scrapped in 1975.

Wartime modifications: *Essex* was commissioned with the standard eight 40mm quadruple mounts, five radio masts, and no hangar catapult. The SK radar was fitted forward on the radar platform. In her April 1944 refit, *Essex* had her bridge modified (deleting one 40mm quadruple) and a second deck catapult was added. The radar platform was enlarged to accommodate the SM and SC-2 radars, while the SK radar was moved to the starboard side of the stack. Two port side hangar deck 40mm quadruples and two quadruples on the starboard quarter were added

Essex during the Okinawa campaign in May 1945 with her late war air group. Between F6F Hellcats and F4U Corsairs (both visible on deck), over 70 percent of the air group was made up of fighters. Note the modified bridge.

(with the last two being placed on inboard positions with a restricted field of fire), making a total of 11 quadruple mounts. In 1945, an SK-2 was fitted. This was her final configuration; she was the only *Essex* class ship never to receive a second stern quadruple, the only ship to retain all five radio masts, and the only ship of the original eight ships in the class never to carry a 40mm quadruple on an outboard sponson.

Yorktown (CV-10)

Built by Newport News and commissioned on May 15, 1943, this ship was originally named *Bon Homme Richard*, but her name was changed to commemorate the sunken *Yorktown* (CV-5). Actually the third *Essex* to be commissioned, she was rushed to service by her eccentric and aggressive first skipper "Jocko" Clark and was the first in her class to see action, with *Essex*, during the Marcus Island raid. She participated in the Truk raid and Philippine Sea. *Yorktown* missed Leyte Gulf but returned in January 1945 to cover the last phases of the Philippines campaign, the Iwo Jima and Okinawa invasions, and the final raids on Japan. The ship was bombed on March 18, 1945, but damage was minor. She was decommissioned in January 1947, but returned to service in 1953 after modernization. *Yorktown* saw three tours of duty off Vietnam. She was finally decommissioned in 1970 but is preserved as a museum ship in Charleston, South Carolina.

Wartime modifications: *Yorktown* was commissioned with an identical configuration to *Essex* but with the hangar catapult fitted. She received a second deck catapult and two starboard quarter 40mm quadruple mounts in December 1943. During her August–October 1944 refit, she received the modified bridge – one 40mm quadruple mount was removed, and eight 40mm quadruple mounts were added for the short-hull maximum quadruple mount fit of 17. *Yorktown* was commissioned with 50 20mm guns; she had 55 by September 1943 and 61 by December 1944. In July 1945 she retained 38 single and 19 double 20mm mounts. For radar, *Yorktown* was commissioned with the SK on the radar platform and the SC-2 on a sponson on the starboard side of the stack. Two SG radars were fitted. After the 1944 refit, the SM was placed on the radar platform and the SK moved to a platform on the port side of the stack. The SC-2 and two SGs were retained. In May 1945, an SK-2 replaced the SK radar. Three radio masts were removed, leaving only the two most forward masts. Several whip antennae were fitted on the starboard quarter; this arrangement became standard for *Essex* class radio mast modifications.

Hornet after her 1945 yard period during which the ship reverted to a Measure 12 two-tone scheme. Evident in this view are the five starboard side sponsons for 40mm quadruple mounts. These sponsons were detachable to permit Panama Canal transits.

A fine study of *Franklin* as she was commissioned in February 1944. The radio masts were brought into an upright position when flight operations were not underway. Many of the galleries for 20mm guns alongside the flight deck are visible. The outrigger for the hangar catapult is also visible in its upright position just aft of the port side 5in guns.

Intrepid (CV-11)

Built by Newport News and commissioned on August 16, 1943, *Intrepid* arrived at Pearl Harbor on January 10, 1944, and saw her first action during the January 1944 raid on Kwajalein. During the raid on Truk, *Intrepid* was torpedoed on February 17 on her starboard quarter 15ft (4.5m) below the waterline. Because of this damage, she missed Philippine Sea but returned to action against Palau in September 1944. *Intrepid* participated in the battle of Leyte Gulf and suffered minor kamikaze damage on October 30. On November 25, she suffered severe damage off Luzon when she was struck by two kamikazes and was forced to return to the US for repairs. The ship returned to action in March 1945 and off Okinawa on April 16, 1945, was again hit by a kamikaze that penetrated into the hangar deck, forcing another return to the US. *Intrepid* was the most often damaged *Essex* class carrier of the war. She had actually returned to service by August just before end of war, demonstrating the toughness of her class. Decommissioned like most other *Essex* class ships in 1947, she returned to service in 1954 after modernization. *Intrepid* saw extensive service off Vietnam (three tours) and was decommissioned in 1974. She is now preserved in New York City.

Wartime modifications: When commissioned, *Intrepid* was identical to *Yorktown* but was fitted with only four radio masts. Before leaving the shipyard, her SK radar was moved from the radar platform to a platform on the starboard side of the stack, which allowed the placement of an SM radar. The SC-2 radar was moved to a platform on the port side of the stack. The SG radar was placed on the topmast with the YE homing beacon. During *Intrepid*'s March–June 1944 repair period, extensive modifications were also made. The bridge was modified and all possible 40mm quadruple mounts were added except the second stern quadruple, for a total of 16 mounts. The hangar deck catapult was removed and the second deck catapult added. The radar platform was lengthened to permit installation of the SK on the rear portion. The SC-2 was moved to the starboard side of the stack. A new pole mast with an enlarged platform was added to the rear of the stack to permit a second SG antenna to be fitted. A short repair period in early 1945 permitted the installation of the second 40mm stern quadruple. Also in 1945, the 20mm battery was modified from the original 55 single guns to 38 single mounts and 19 twin mounts. The ship retained four radio masts.

Hornet (CV-12)

Built by Newport News, *Hornet* was the seventh ship of the class actually completed, and was commissioned on November 29, 1943. She was originally named *Kearsarge*, but was renamed *Hornet* to honor CV-8, lost in October 1942 in the battle of Santa Cruz. *Hornet*'s first action was at Philippine Sea; she served through Leyte Gulf and the raids on Japan. Her only major damage during the war was in June 1945, when a typhoon buckled the forward flight deck. Decommissioned in January

1947, she returned to service in 1953 and saw action off Vietnam. *Hornet* was decommissioned in 1970 and is preserved in Alameda, California.

Wartime modifications: When commissioned, the ship was fitted with the early bridge, a hangar catapult, four radio masts, and ten quadruple mounts (the standard eight plus the two starboard quarter mounts). The SK radar was moved to the rear of the radar platform to permit installation of an SM set. The ship remained in this configuration until her July–September 1945 refit following typhoon damage. During this yard period, the bridge was modified, the hangar deck catapult removed, and a second deck catapult fitted. Eight more quadruple 40mm mounts were fitted for a final total of 17. The SK-2 replaced the SK and was fitted on the radar platform. This made her the only *Essex* class to carry the SK-2 dish on the radar platform; all other ships placed the SK-2 outboard of the stack.

Franklin (CV-13)

Built by Newport News and commissioned on January 31,1944, she was the eighth *Essex* completed. She participated in Philippine Sea and the Philippines campaign. *Franklin* was damaged by kamikaze attack off Luzon on October 15, 1944, and again on October 30, 1944. The ship suffered the most extensive damage of any *Essex* class carrier off Kyushu on March 19, 1945, when she was struck by two 550lb (250kg) bombs that penetrated into the hangar deck and ignited aircraft being fueled and armed. The ship was saved by extraordinary damage control efforts but at the cost of 724 crewmen killed and 256 wounded. *Franklin* was not repaired before the end of the war and was decommissioned in February 1947. Due to her severe wartime damage, she was never returned to service or modernized and was scrapped in 1966.

Wartime modifications: As commissioned, the ship had the same configuration as *Hornet*. In May 1944, the bridge was modified and the hangar deck catapult removed at Norfolk before she departed for the Pacific. The ship returned to the US in December 1944 for repairs following kamikaze damage. During this time she received a second deck catapult, and the SK radar was moved to the aft position on the radar platform. Commissioned with eight 40mm quadruples, she completed this refit with a final total of 17 quadruple 40mm mounts. She was also fitted with an SK-2 radar on the starboard side of the stack.

Ticonderoga (CV-14)

Built by Newport News and commissioned on May 8, 1944, *Ticonderoga* was the tenth *Essex* class to be completed and the second long-hull unit to

Ticonderoga on January 12, 1945, off Formosa. On this day, two kamikazes hit the ship. In this view, the fires have been brought under control, but fire damage to the forward part of the island is evident from the second kamikaze hit. The ship is in a Measure 33/10a scheme.

enter service. Her combat career began during the Philippines campaign and she received her only war damage on January 21, 1945, off Formosa, when two kamikazes caused severe damage, killing 143 crewmen and wounding 202. She was repaired in time to reenter service by April 1945. *Ticonderoga* was decommissioned in January 1947, but was modernized and returned to service. She again saw combat service off Vietnam. The ship was decommissioned for the last time in 1973 and scrapped in 1974.

Wartime modifications: *Ticonderoga* was completed with two deck catapults and a modified bridge. She began her career with a total of 11 quadruple mounts, including the second bow and stern mounts and two on the port side hangar deck sponson. Her original radar fit included an SM on the forward portion of the radar platform, with the SK mounted on the rear of the platform (she was the last *Essex* built with an SK) and the SC-2 fitted on the starboard platform off the stack. One SG was also fitted. During the ship's early 1945 refit, an SK-2 was added on a platform on the starboard side of the stack and a second SG was fitted on the aft mast. Seven additional 40mm quadruples were fitted for the long-hull maximum of 18. By 1945, the 20mm battery had been reduced to 35 guns.

Randolph (CV-15)

Built by Newport News, *Randolph* was a long-hull unit, the 13th *Essex* class carrier to be completed, and was commissioned on October 9, 1944. She saw combat service during the Iwo Jima operation and the 1945 raids on Japan. On March 11, 1945, she was hit by a kamikaze while anchored at Ulithi, but was quickly repaired. After the war she was decommissioned in June 1947, but was modernized and returned to service in 1953. She was ultimately decommissioned in 1969 and sold for scrap in 1973.

Wartime modifications: Built late in the war, she was commissioned with two deck catapults, the modified bridge and an SK-2 radar. Upon completion, she shipped 11 quadruple 40mm mounts and 57 20mm guns. In January 1945, another seven quadruple mounts were added, for a final total of 18.

Randolph was struck on March 11, 1945 by a single kamikaze while anchored in Ulithi Atoll. In this view she is pictured alongside a repair ship two days later. Despite appearances, the damage was quickly repaired at Ulithi.

Lexington (CV-16)

Originally named *Cabot*, she was renamed to honor CV-2, sunk at the battle of Coral Sea in May 1942. Built by Bethlehem Quincy and commissioned on March 17, 1943, *Lexington* was actually the second *Essex* to be commissioned. Her first action was during the Gilbert Islands invasion, but she was torpedoed by aircraft soon thereafter on December 4, 1943, off Kwajalein. *Lexington* returned to participate in Philippine Sea and at Leyte Gulf. Damaged by kamikaze attack off Luzon on November 5, 1944, she returned to service for the Iwo Jima operation and the final raids on Japan. The ship was decommissioned in April 1947. Brought back into service in 1955, she was designated a training carrier in 1962. *Lexington* lasted in this role until 1991, becoming the longest serving *Essex* class ship. She is preserved in Corpus Christi, Texas.

Lexington in November 1943 after having recovered from an air strike. The ship appears in her early configuration with five radio masts (lowered for flight operations), an unmodified bridge, and no outboard starboard side sponsons. The two 40mm quadruple mounts located on the aft starboard portion of the hangar deck were later moved into sponsons to increase their fields of fire.

Wartime modifications: *Lexington* was completed with the standard eight quadruple mounts, the standard early radar fit, no hangar catapult, and five radio masts. The second deck catapult was added in December 1943 during repairs for battle damage; seven (mostly sponson-mounted) 40mm quadruples were also added. Her radar fit in early 1944 included an SM on the forward portion of the radar platform, an SG on the topmast, an SK placed on the starboard side of the stack, and the SC-2 on the port side. A second SG was mounted aft of the stack to cover the rear blind spot. Her final refit in May 1945 added an SK-2 radar, replaced the SC-2 set with an SR, and added the second stern quadruple 40mm and the two quadruple mounts on the port side flight deck platforms. After the bridge was modified, the final quadruple mount fit was 17. By March 1945, her light antiaircraft fit included 25 twin 20mm mounts, and six Army quadruple .50-cal. machine guns were fitted in March 1945.

Bunker Hill (CV-17)

Built by Bethlehem Quincy and commissioned on May 24, 1943, *Bunker Hill* was the fourth *Essex* to be completed. Her combat career began in November 1943 with strikes against Rabaul and she remained in action through 1944. After returning from a refit, she suffered severe damage from kamikazes off Okinawa on May 11, 1945. The two hits resulted in deadly fires that left 346 crewmen dead – the most severe damage except for that suffered by *Franklin*. Repaired by July 1945, she saw no more combat service. *Bunker Hill* was decommissioned in January 1947 and was never modernized. She was used as an experimental ship until 1973, when she was finally sent for scrapping.

Wartime modifications: *Bunker Hill* was completed with the standard eight quadruple mounts, a standard early radar fit, and a hangar catapult. She remained in this configuration until a refit in early 1945 during which a second deck catapult was added, the bridge was modified, and additional 40mm quadruples were added to bring her up to the short-hull maximum of 17.

Wasp (CV-18)

Originally named *Oriskany*, *Wasp* was renamed in honor of CV-7, lost in August 1942. Built by Bethlehem Quincy, she was the sixth *Essex* completed and was commissioned on November 24, 1943. Her first combat action was during the Hollandia operation and she remained in action for the rest of the war, earning eight battle stars. She suffered slight damage from a bombing attack off Kyushu on March 19, 1945, and in

A: USS *Yorktown* (CV-10), early configuration

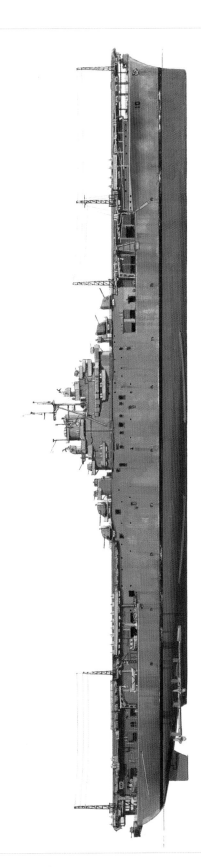

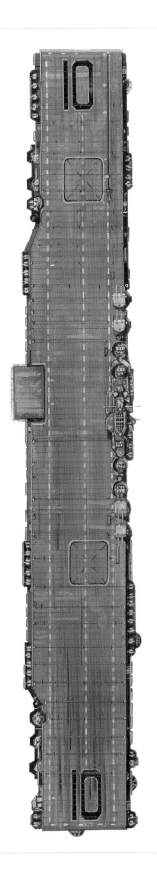

B

B: USS *Lexington* (CV-16), late war configuration

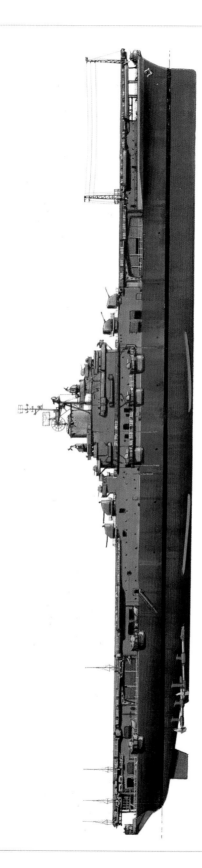
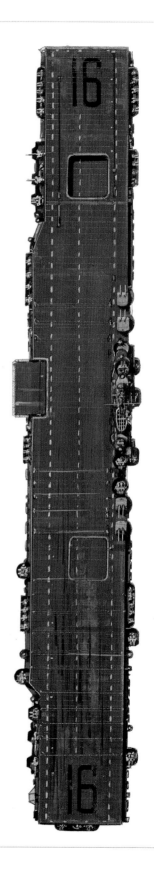

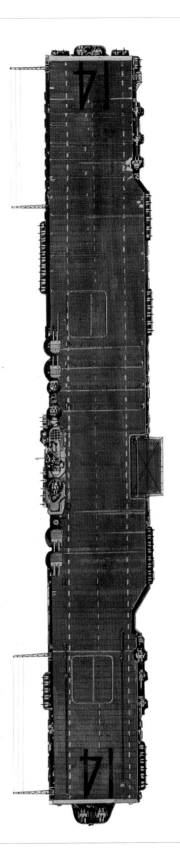

D: USS *ESSEX*, AUGUST 1943

KEY

1 Catapult
2 Radio masts
3 20mm single gun mounts
4 Forward elevator
5 Hangar deck roller curtains
6 Dual 5-inch/38 gun mounts
7 Mark 51 directors
8 Mark 4 40mm Bofors quad gun mounts
9 Flag plot
10 Navigating Bridge
11 Pilot House
12 Primary Fly control station

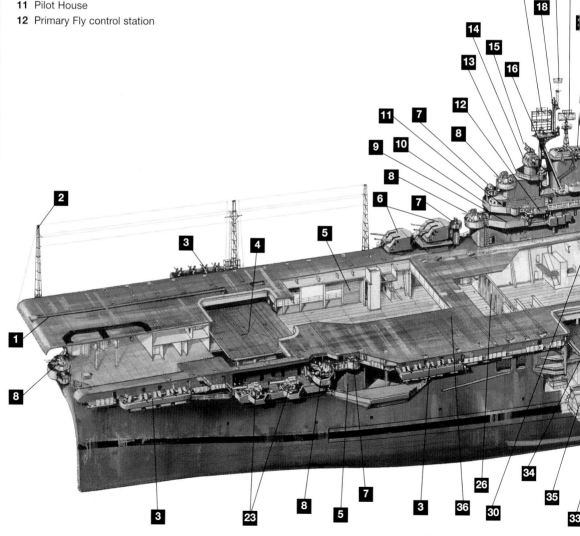

13 Island
14 Mark 37 directors
15 Mark 4 radar
16 Radar platform
17 SK radar
18 SG radar
19 YE Antenna
20 SC-2 radar
21 Smoke stack
22 Battle gaff
23 Single 5in Mk 40 Mounts
24 Propellers (4-blade) and shafts

25 Hangar deck
26 Hangar deck fire curtains
27 Aft elevator
28 No 2 Engine Room
29 No 4 Fire (boiler) Room
30 Boiler uptake casings
31 No 3 Fire Room
32 No 1 Engine Room
33 No 2 Fire Room
34 Deck edge elevator
35 No 1 Fire Room
36 Flight deck

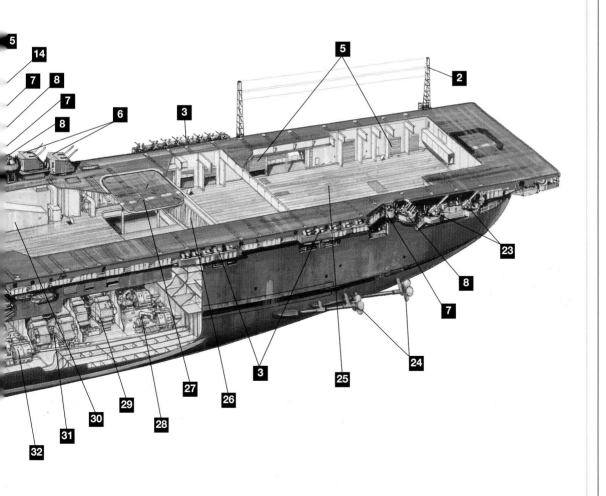

E: The *Independence* class carriers

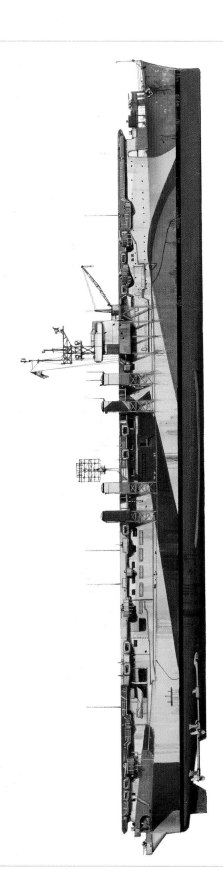

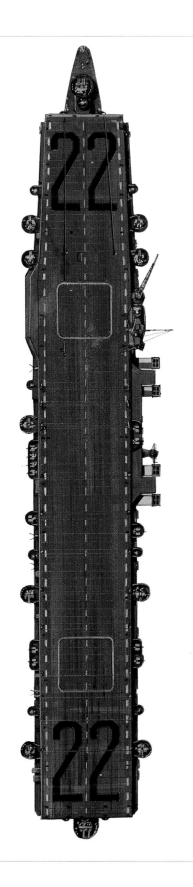

F: Kamikazes attack *Intrepid*, November 25, 1944

F

G: *Princeton* is bombed, October 24, 1944

August sustained forward flight deck damage from a typhoon. *Wasp* was decommissioned in February 1947, but was back in commission by 1951. The ship was decommissioned for the final time in 1972 and scrapped.

Wartime modifications: As commissioned, *Wasp* was fitted with a hangar catapult and ten quadruple mounts, and her SK radar was placed on a platform on the starboard side of the stack. During her June 1945 refit, a second deck catapult was added, the bridge was modified, and the second stern, two port side hangar decks, three starboard side sponsons, and the two port side flight deck quadruple mounts were all fitted for a final configuration of 17 quadruple mounts. The two aft radio masts and the hangar catapult were removed and the SK remained on the starboard side of stack.

Hancock (CV-19)

Built by Bethlehem Quincy and commissioned on April 15, 1944, *Hancock* was the first long hull to be commissioned and the ninth *Essex* overall. Her first major combat action was Leyte Gulf; she participated in the remainder of the Philippines campaign and then covered the Iwo Jima invasion. She was damaged on January 21, 1945, by an unexplained aviation gas explosion, and on April 7, 1945, by a kamikaze, which forced her to miss the rest of the war. Decommissioned in May 1947, *Hancock* returned to service in 1954 after modernization. She conducted seven tours off Vietnam, making her the most active of the war-built *Essex* class carriers. *Hancock* was finally decommissioned in 1976 and scrapped.

Wartime modifications: *Hancock* was commissioned with several improvements already integrated. These included the modified bridge, two deck catapults, two stern quadruple mounts, two quadruple mounts on the clipper bow, and the two quadruple mounts placed off the forward port side of the hangar. The SK radar was placed on the aft position of the radar platform. During repairs for battle damage in June 1945, she had her 40mm battery augmented with the addition of five starboard side sponsons and two on the port side flight deck platforms, for a final total of 18.

Hancock in April 1944 just after being commisioned. She is in a Measure 32/3a scheme. The clipper bow of this long-hull unit is apparent, as are the two 40mm quadruples fitted on the bow.

Bennington (CV-20)

Built by the New York Navy Yard in Brooklyn, *Bennington* was the 11th *Essex* completed. Commissioned on August 6, 1944, she arrived in the Pacific in time to participate in the Iwo Jima operation, and in April 1945 her aircraft contributed to the sinking of the *Yamato*. She suffered damage similar to that of *Hornet* during a June 1945 typhoon. Decommissioned in November 1946, she was back in service in 1952 following modernization. After serving three tours off Vietnam, she was decommissioned in 1970 and was sold for scrap in 1994.

Wartime modifications: *Bennington* was the first short-hull unit completed with major improvements built in. She was finished with the late war bridge, two deck catapults, an SM and an SK-2 on the radar platform (the first SK-2 fitted on a short-hull unit) and ten quadruple mounts (the standard seven plus a second on the stern and two port side hangar deck mounts). When she arrived in the Pacific, *Bennington* was rushed into combat to replace heavy carrier losses from the Okinawa campaign and she did not have any other quadruple mounts fitted before the end of the war.

Bon Homme Richard (CV-31)

Built by the New York Navy Yard, *Bon Homme Richard* was the last short-hull unit completed in time to see war service. Commissioned on November 26, 1944, she arrived in the Pacific to participate in the final raids on the Japanese Home Islands. After her brief war service, she was decommissioned in January 1947. Following modernization, she was recommissioned in 1951 and saw service off both Korea and Vietnam. The ship was finally decommissioned in 1971 and sold for scrap in 1992.

Wartime modifications: Since she was the 14th *Essex* completed, she entered service with late war modifications already incorporated, including the modified bridge, two deck catapults and an SK-2. She was commissioned with ten quadruple 40mm mounts (as on *Bennington*), and another seven were added in May 1945 en route to the war zone (the five starboard side sponsons and the two port side flight deck platform mounts).

Shangri-La (CV-38)

This long-hull ship was built by Norfolk Navy Yard and commissioned on September 15, 1944. She was the 12th *Essex* completed, arriving in time to participate in the final raids on Japan. Decommissioned in November

1947, she was returned to service in 1955. The ship served off Vietnam before being decommissioned in 1971 and sold for scrap in 1988.

Wartime modifications: As completed, the ship has a late war configuration of two deck catapults, the modified bridge, and the first SK-2 radar fitted on a long-hull ship. She entered service with 11 quadruple 40mm mounts – the standard seven plus an additional mount on the bow and stern, and the two on the forward port side hangar deck. *Shangri-La* had no modifications during her short war service.

In addition to the 14 ships that saw wartime service, another three were commissioned in 1945 but did not arrive in time to see active service. These were all long-hull ships and included *Boxer* (CV-21), *Antietam* (CV-36), and *Lake Champlain* (CV-39). *Antietam* was actually present at the Japanese surrender in September 1945. Additional ships were completed after the war in 1945 and during 1946, including *Leyte* (CV-32), *Kearsarge* (CV-33), *Princeton* (CV-37), *Tarawa* (CV-40), *Valley Force* (CV-45), and *Philippine Sea* (CV-47). The final ship to enter service was *Oriskany* (CV-34), which was completed in 1950 to a modified design.

Assessment

It is hard to overstate the importance of the *Essex* class to the US Navy's Pacific campaign. The class was the most numerous of any US fleet carrier (in fact, of any fleet carrier in history), a fact that pays testimony to the utility of the basic design and to the productiveness of American shipyards. Designed before the war, the carriers proved able to accommodate

wartime requirements and modifications. While the design was far from perfect, and numerous wartime additions made the ships dangerously top heavy, this potential weakness was never tested. By 1945, the carriers were very overcrowded. Nevertheless, with their large air group, high speed, and great endurance, these were the ships that broke the back of the Imperial Japanese Navy and carried the war to the Japanese homeland itself.

ESSEX CLASS

Displacement: standard 27,500 tons (24,948 tonnes)
full load 36,380 tons (33,003 tonnes)
Dimensions:
Length 872ft (265.8m) (888ft [270.6m] for long hull)
Beam 93ft (28.3m)
Draft 27.5ft (8.4m) (full load)
Maximum speed: 33kt (61.1km/h)
Radius: 15,440nm at 15kt (28,595km at 27.8km/h)
Crew: 3,448 (service)

THE *INDEPENDENCE* CLASS

Origins

The *Independence* class was a crash conversion program brought about by wartime expediency. In 1941, it appeared that the lead ship of the *Essex* class would not be delivered until early 1944. The idea behind the *Independence* class was a program to bridge that gap. The person pushing the concept was none other than President Roosevelt, who proposed using some of the *Cleveland* class light cruisers for conversion into light carriers. The Navy had already considered several schemes for carrier conversions, but rejected Roosevelt's proposals on the grounds that the ships could not be completed before the expected arrival of the *Essex* class units, and, when completed on a light cruiser hull, would be inferior units. The conversions that the Navy had in mind were much more complex than anything that Roosevelt envisioned, so the early rejection of his proposals is not surprising. Roosevelt insisted that the Navy consider a more austere conversion, and in October 1941 the Navy agreed that a light carrier conversion could be completed more quickly if design limitations were accepted. On this basis, and in accordance with Roosevelt's wishes, the first conversion was ordered in January 1942 using one hull, and by June 1942 the conversion program had grown to nine of the 36 planned *Cleveland* class light cruisers.

With a displacement of some 10,000 tons (9,072 tonnes) and a waterline length of 600ft (182.9m), the *Cleveland* class cruisers were the smallest hulls that the Navy considered suitable for conversion into a carrier with a useful air group and the speed to operate with the fleet. However, the use of a light cruiser hull would result in many problems and would not culminate in a ship optimized for flight operations. The narrow hull would constrain the size of the hangar and flight deck and the latter would be further restricted by an island. Additionally, the sheer of the cruiser hull also provided problems for the placement of aircraft elevators and the construction of the hangar deck, which obviously required a level deck. To overcome these problems, it was decided that a flight deck short of the bow was acceptable. An island was included in the

Princeton **was launched on October 18, 1942, at Camden, New Jersey. Her cruiser lines are quite evident, as is the potential for future instability problems as weaponry and equipment are fitted at the ship's flight deck level.**

final design, but it was a small one (similar to escort carriers) and was built outside the line of the flight deck. The sheer of the cruiser hull meant that in order to maintain the structural strength of the main deck the new hangar deck was built 4ft (1.2m) above the main deck, and that elevators were placed farther aft, though this was not optimum for flight deck operations. All nine ships were built at New York Shipbuilding in Camden, New Jersey. Five ships were laid down as *Cleveland* class cruisers and the last four as carriers. All were commissioned in 1943, with the building time reduced to a mere 13.5 months for the last ship of the class.

Design and construction

The cruiser hull was completed up to the main deck. With displacement increasing to 11,000 tons (9,979 tonnes) and much of the weight located high up on the ship, the hulls were blistered (widened) to increase stability. The blisters were also used to increase fuel stowage.

Originally the ships were designed without an island. However, fleet experience demonstrated the advantages of even a small island, so one was later added and a radar mast incorporated. The small escort carrier-sized island was built entirely outside the line of the flight deck and hull in order to ease aircraft-handling problems. Only a pilot house and a chart house were contained in the island. The CIC and the radar control rooms were on the gallery deck. Just forward of the island was an aircraft crane to lift aircraft from the pier to the flight deck. This flight deck level crane was required as it would be impossible to lift planes to the enclosed hangar deck. Disposal of exhaust gases was conducted by venting each of the four boilers through a separate small stack arranged on the starboard side aft of the small island. To counterbalance the small island, the crane, and the four small funnels, 82 tons (74.4 tonnes) of concrete ballast was added to the port side tanks.

Armor was minimal and there was no flight deck protection. The main armored deck was only 2in (5.1cm) thick, while the main belt was a maximum of 5in (12.7cm), tapering to 3¼in (8.3cm) of armor (the first two ships in the class had no belt protection because of a shortage of armor). Bulkheads over magazines and steering gear were as much as 5in (12.7cm) deep. The torpedo storage area was given additional splinter protection and bomb elevators and ammunition hoists also received additional protection.

The original *Cleveland* class machinery was retained, which produced 100,000 shaft horsepower using four Babcock and Wilcox boilers, each driving a General Electric turbine. This rendered a top speed of 31 knots (57.4km/h) – sufficient for fleet work, but not equal to the *Essex* class units. Range was half that of the *Essex* units but still proved adequate.

Armament

The *Independence* class was the only class of US carrier fitted with entirely automatic weapons. The lead ship of the class was originally fitted with a 5in/38 single mount on the bow and the stern to counter surface attack. At the request of the *Independence*'s commanding

This starboard bow shot of *Langley* clearly shows the hull lines of the *Cleveland* class cruiser upon which the conversion of the *Independence* class was based. The placement of the island and the four small smoke funnels outside of the lines of the hull is also evident.

officer, these were replaced by 40mm quadruple mounts after only six weeks.

In addition to the two quadruple 40mm mounts, standard weapons fit for the *Independence* class was eight twin 40mm and 14 20mm guns. In February 1943, approval was given for a ninth twin 40mm mount that was added on the forward port side of the flight deck. Only *Independence* was completed with just eight 40mm mounts; the other eight ships received all nine twin mounts before completion. Seven Mark 51 Directors were fitted to provide fire control for the 20mm and 40mm batteries.

Standard radar fit for the light carriers included an SK air search radar between the two groups of small smoke stacks on the starboard side, with an SC-2 radar in the radar mast. The wide separation of these two radars made for a better radar performance than that of the *Essex* class, where the closely grouped radars suffered from mutual interference. An SG surface search radar was also fitted on the radar mast and a YE aircraft homing beacon on the topmast.

This close-up of the island on *Cowpens* shows the small size of *Independence* class islands. The large radar is the SC-2 and above that is the SG surface search radar. The radar-looking device on the top of the topmast is actually the YE aircraft homing beacon. The circular devices are loudspeakers.

Aircraft-handling facilities

The flight deck was 552ft (168.2m) long and 73ft (22.2m) wide. Originally, a single flush deck catapult was fitted. There were two centerline elevators. Extra space was provided on the flight deck by the forward elevator so that aircraft could bypass the elevator. Eight arresting gear wires were fitted aft; these were the same type found on the *Essex* class. The hangar was limited in size and width, being only 285ft (86.9m) long and 55ft (16.8m) wide.

Aviation ordnance storage was not generous. A total of 331 tons (300 tonnes) of aviation ordnance could be carried, with the original cruiser magazines converted to store bombs. Seventy-two each 1,000lb (454kg) and 500lb (227kg) bombs were carried. A space aft of the hangar was converted to store 24 torpedoes. Aviation gas capacity was 122,000 gallons (461,820 liters).

The light carrier's air group was originally to be mixed and was a reduced version of a fleet carrier air group. This mixed group was to include 24 F4F Wildcat fighters, 12 Dauntless dive bombers, and nine Avenger torpedo planes. When the larger F6F Hellcat replaced the Wildcat, fewer fighters could be carried, so in October 1943 the light carrier air group was reduced to 12 fighters, nine dive bombers, and nine torpedo planes. Dauntless dive bombers with their non-folding wings were soon discarded, and by November 1943 the air group was set at 25 Hellcats and nine Avengers. Frequently during the war the light carrier air groups were tasked to provide Combat Air Patrol (CAP) over the task group, freeing the larger fleet carrier air groups to focus on strike missions. In accordance with this *de facto* doctrine, proposals were made throughout the war to make the *Independence* class into all-fighter carriers. Just

Independence viewed from the stern in July 1943. The stern 5in gun has already been exchanged for a much more useful quadruple 40mm mount.

Independence **viewed from the bow in July 1943. The bow 5in gun has been removed and has been replaced with a quadruple 40mm mount. Two additional bow-mounted 20mm single mounts were also fitted.**

before the end of the war this was approved and the air group was set at 36 Hellcat or Corsair fighters. However, only a single carrier, *Cabot*, saw action with an all-fighter air group. In 1944, *Independence* was assigned duties as a night carrier with an air group of 19 F6F-5N Hellcat fighters and eight TBM-1D Avenger bombers. Night carrier duties were later assumed by the larger fleet carriers that could more safely conduct night flight operations.

Wartime modifications

Modifications were largely restricted to upgrading the antiaircraft armament. As completed, *Independence* had 14 20mm guns. The number of 20mm mounts was increased to 22 on some ships by adding new platforms along the flight deck. Later, the single mounts were replaced with five twin mounts (six in *Monterey*). Increasing top-weight problems required the deletion of some of the 20mm mounts, including the mounts on the bow and stern. It proved impossible to fit more 40mm guns in place of the ineffective 20mm mounts owing to weight problems. During their refits, some ships exchanged some of their Mark 51 Directors for the Mark 57 Director.

In 1944 the radar fit was modified when the back-up SC-2 air search radar on the front part of the radar mast was deleted in favor of a height-finder radar. *Independence* received the SM radar and other units (except *Princeton*) the lighter SP set.

Operational histories

Independence (CVL-22)

Independence was laid down as the cruiser *Amsterdam* in May 1941. The ship was commissioned in January 1943 and first saw action in the Marcus Island raid. The ship remained active until torpedoed and severely damaged by Japanese aircraft in November 1943 during the Gilbert Islands invasion. *Independence* missed the first half of 1944, returning in time for the Philippines invasion and Leyte Gulf. She remained in action for the rest of the war, earning a total of eight battle stars. Four different air groups were deployed aboard her, including a night air group between September 1944 and January 1945. After the war, *Independence* was used in the atomic tests at Bikini Atoll in 1946. The ship was decommissioned in August 1946 following heavy test damage and was used as a weapons trials ship until sunk as a target in 1951.

Princeton (CVL-23)

Princeton was the only ship of the class destined to be lost in action. She was laid down as the cruiser *Tallahassee* in June 1941. The ship was commissioned in January 1943 and first saw action in the Tarawa raid in September 1943. She remained in action through the Truk raid and Philippine Sea. During the battle for Leyte Gulf, on October 24, she was struck by a single 550lb (250kg) bomb from a land-based Japanese aircraft. The bomb penetrated the flight and hangar decks to explode on the main armor deck. The ensuing fire spread to the hangar deck, where fully fueled aircraft added to the blaze. The efforts of the fire-fighting teams appeared to be paying off until the fire reached the torpedo stowage area aft of the hangar deck. The explosion of the remaining torpedoes wrecked the carrier and also inflicted severe topside damage to a cruiser, which was alongside to assist in the fire-fighting effort. *Princeton* was later scuttled. Besides being the only ship of her class to be destroyed, she was the last US non-escort fleet carrier lost during the war.

Belleau Wood (CVL-24)

Belleau Wood was originally laid down as the cruiser *New Haven* in August 1941; she was commissioned in March 1943. *Belleau Wood*'s first action was during the Tarawa raid. She was present for most of the Fast Carrier Force's actions, including the Truk raid, Philippine Sea, and Leyte Gulf. During the battle of the Philippine Sea, her torpedo bombers sank the Japanese carrier *Hiyo*, the only Japanese carrier sunk by air attack in the battle. Following Leyte Gulf, the ship was damaged by a kamikaze on October 30, 1944. Following repairs and refit, *Belleau Wood* returned in February 1945 to support the Okinawa invasion and to take part in the raids on Japan. She earned a total of 12 battle stars and was the second most active ship of her class, with 17 months of active operations. Decommissioned in 1947, she was loaned to France in 1953 and renamed *Bois Belleau*. After being returned in 1960, she was scrapped two years later.

Cowpens (CVL-25)

Cowpens was laid down as the cruiser *Huntington* in November 1941. Commissioned in May 1943, she first saw action in the October 1943 Wake Island raid. *Cowpens* went on to earn 12 battle stars, participating in all fast carrier major operations except Okinawa, when she was in refit. By the war's conclusion, she was the most active of her class, spending 18 of her 24 months in the Pacific in active service. In spite of this, she was undamaged by enemy action, but did suffer damage in the typhoon of December 1944. *Cowpens* was decommissioned in 1947 and never returned to service. The ship was scrapped in 1962.

Monterey (CVL-26)

Monterey was originally begun as the cruiser *Dayton* in December 1941. Commissioned in June 1943, she reached the Pacific in time to participate in the Gilbert Islands operation in November 1943. *Monterey* went on to earn 11 battle stars, including service at Truk, Philippine Sea, Leyte Gulf, Okinawa, and the final raids on Japan. Her wartime service was interrupted after she was damaged in the December 1944 typhoon and was forced to return to the US for repairs. She returned in time for the operations off Okinawa and the final strikes against Japan. Decommissioned in 1947, she was reactivated in 1950 and employed as a training carrier until 1955. This made her one of the few light carriers to be employed by the US Navy after the war – in general, their small size made them unsuitable for most aircraft in service. The ship was finally scrapped in 1970.

Bataan off the Philadelphia Navy Yard in early March 1944 before departing for the Pacific. The 40mm quadruple mount fitted on the bow is clearly shown, as are several 20mm single mounts. Two dual 40mm mounts are shown on the starboard side forward of the island. The size of the larger quadruple mounts meant that they could only be fitted on the bow and stern of the light carriers.

Langley (CVL-27)

Langley was authorized as the cruiser *Fargo* in March 1942. The ship was later given the carrier name *Crown Point* but was eventually renamed *Langley* in honor of the former US aircraft carrier CV-1 sunk by the Japanese in February 1942. She was commissioned in August 1943 and saw her first action during the occupation of Kwajalein in January 1944. *Langley* remained in action until May 1945, when she went into refit, missing the last stages of the war. The ship earned a total of nine battle stars. Her only wartime damage was slight bomb damage in January 1945. Decommissioned in 1947, *Langley* was loaned to France in 1951 and renamed *Lafayette*. She was finally scrapped in 1964, following her return in 1963.

Cabot (CVL-28)

Cabot was destined to be the longest serving *Independence* class ship. She was laid down as the cruiser *Wilmington* in March 1942 and commissioned in July 1943. *Cabot*'s first combat operation was during the occupation of Kwajalein in the Marshall Islands in January 1944. She subsequently participated in the Truk raid, Philippine Sea, Leyte Gulf, and through the early parts of the Okinawa campaign, but departed in April for a refit. Her only wartime damage was from a kamikaze strike off Luzon in November 1944. Decommissioned in 1947, she was recommissioned in 1948 and served through 1955 as a training carrier. Her second career began in 1967, when she was loaned to Spain and renamed *Dedalo*. Later, in 1972, she was sold to the Spanish, and remained in service until 1989. She was returned to the US, but efforts to preserve her unfortunately proved unsuccessful and the ship was scrapped in 2000.

Bataan (CVL-29)

Bataan was ordered as the cruiser *Buffalo* and laid down as a carrier in August 1942. Commissioned in November 1943, her first action was the Hollandia operation in April 1944. She subsequently participated in Philippine Sea but missed Leyte Gulf during her only war refit period. The ship returned to service to support the Okinawa invasion and to participate in the raids on Japan. *Bataan* was decommissioned in 1947 but was brought back into service in 1950 and conducted three deployments off Korea, thus becoming the only *Independence* class light

carrier to see combat action with the US Navy after the Second World War. Decommissioned for the last time in 1954, she was scrapped in 1959.

San Jacinto (CVL-30)

San Jacinto was authorized as the light cruiser *Newark* in October 1942 and was the last ship of her class to be commissioned in December 1943. She arrived in the Pacific to take part in Philippine Sea and saw continual action thereafter, earning five battle stars and a Presidential Unit Citation. In late August 1945, *San Jacinto* departed the war zone for refit. Decommissioned in 1947, the ship never saw service again, being scrapped in 1979.

Assessment

The quick conversion of the nine *Independence* class ships was a significant achievement. Even with their small air groups, the nine ships represented the equivalent aircraft capacity of approximately four fleet carriers. Keeping in mind that they entered service before the expected 1944 arrival of the *Essex* class ships, the *Independence* class was a significant insurance policy. This proved especially important given the heavy attrition of the prewar-built carriers during 1942. On the minus side, the operation of these smaller deck carriers resulted in a much higher accident rate. Their austere design offered speed of completion but also

Monterey at anchor at Ulithi Atoll in November 1944. The ship is in a badly worn Measure 33/3d scheme. Her entire air group is spotted on the flight deck with F6F Hellcats placed on the stern.

Cabot in August 1943 just after commissioning. The ship is in a Measure 21 scheme, which she retained throughout the war, being one of two *Independence* class carriers never to receive a dazzle scheme.

San Jacinto underway off the US east coast in January 1944. The ship is in a Measure 33/7a scheme. She still retains the SC-2 radar mounted on the radar mast.

presented the problems associated with a small air group, lack of flight deck and hangar deck flexibility, increased vulnerability to damage, and uncomfortable living conditions. On balance, the class proved a success and certainly compared favorably to the largely ineffective conversions that constituted the Imperial Japanese Navy's light carriers. Unlike the Japanese conversions, the *Independence* class was armored and properly compartmented, and possessed a speed of over 30 knots (55.6km/h).

INDEPENDENCE CLASS

Displacement: 14,300 tons (12,973 tonnes) full load (except *Independence* and *Princeton*, 14,000 tons [12,701 tonnes])
Dimensions:
    Length 622.6ft (189.8m)
    Beam 71.5ft (21.8m)
    Draft 26ft (7.9m)
Maximum speed: 31kt (57.4km/h)
Radius: 8,325nm at 15kt (15,418km at 27.8km/h)
Crew: originally 140 officers and 1,321 men – increased to 1,569 in service

BIBLIOGRAPHY

Brown, David, *Aircraft Carriers*, Arco Publishing Company, New York (1977)

Campbell, John, *Naval Weapons of World War Two*, Naval Institute Press, Annapolis, Maryland (2002)

Chesneau, Roger, *Aircraft Carriers*, Naval Institute Press, Annapolis, Maryland (1992)

Faltum, Andrew, *The* Essex *Aircraft Carriers*, Nautical and Aviation Publishing Company of America, Charleston, South Carolina (2000)

– *The* Independence *Light Aircraft Carriers*, Nautical and Aviation Publishing Company of America, Charleston, South Carolina (2002)

Friedman, Norman, *U.S. Aircraft Carriers*, Naval Institute Press, Annapolis, Maryland (1983)

Preston, Antony (ed.), *Warship Volume II*, Conway Maritime Press, London (1978)

Reynolds, Clark, *The Fast Carriers*, Naval Institute Press, Annapolis, Maryland (1968)

Sowinski, L., *U.S. Navy Camouflage of the WW2 Era (2)*, The Floating Drydock, Philadelphia (1977)

Williams, David, *Naval Camouflage 1914–1945*, Naval Institute Press, Annapolis, Maryland (2001)

COLOR PLATE COMMENTARY

COLOR SCHEMES

The US Navy made extensive use of ship camouflage during the war. In fact, every *Essex* and *Princeton* class carrier received at least one camouflage scheme during its service, and most were painted in several different schemes during various periods of the war, providing a useful tool in identifying individual ships. The US Navy's Bureau of Ships was responsible for issuing camouflage directions. The June 1942 instructions were the last set of camouflage patterns (called "measures") issued, and these provided the colors and patterns used on *Essex* and *Independence* class ships.

During the war, carrier measures were of two basic types. Many ships were painted in "dazzle" schemes that were intended to confuse an enemy surface observer with regard to the ship's true course and speed. These were primarily designed to defend against submarine attack. There were also several solid color measures designed to reduce the ship's observability from the air. These measures made a strong comeback late in the war as the kamikaze threat grew. Each scheme had a number that identified the measure, the color range, and the design number. For example, Ms (Measure) 32/6a called for the color shades allowed for Ms 32 painted in design 6; the 'a' indicated that the design was prepared for an aircraft carrier. Schemes could be "open," meaning that they did not require a specific color, for example Ms 3_/8a.

The wooden flight decks of all carriers were painted during the war. Originally they were stained with Flight Deck Blue (number 21) but in 1944 a darker stain matching Deck Blue (20-B) was used. There were standard flight deck markings, but these often varied from ship to ship. Starting at the end of 1943, each carrier had its hull number painted on the forward and aft ends of the flight deck in large numbers to assist aviators to identify their home ship. Flight deck numbers were usually painted in Dull Black or Deck Blue. These were sometimes outlined in a light color. Occasionally, the numbers were painted in a light color, either white or yellow. Deck stripes were originally light gray or blue, then changed to yellow after arrival in the Pacific during 1943, and then finally to white. Two or three dashed stripes were applied to the flight deck – one on the centerline and two on the flight deck edges – denoting the safe area for take-off and landings. Markings were also used to indicate the location of the ship's elevators either by outlining them in a lighter color or, more commonly, by placing an "X" over the elevator. One ship (*Intrepid*) was known to have painted false elevator markings in an effort to mislead kamikaze pilots, who were known to aim for the elevators to put the ship's aircraft-handling capacity out of action.

These are the camouflage schemes used by *Essex* and *Independence* class carriers during the war:

Measure 12: This was a graded scheme using Sea Blue 5-S from the waterline to the hangar deck level, Ocean Gray 5-O on all other vertical surfaces, and Haze Gray 5-H on all masts. Flight decks were painted in Deck Blue 20-B. Measure 12 was considered to be effective in its purpose of providing concealment against both surface and aerial observation while also providing some course and range deception.

Measure 14: This scheme was intended to give concealment against surface observation but proved to make the ship more easily observable by aircraft. It consisted of a single color, Ocean Gray. Flight decks were painted in Deck Blue.

Measure 21: This was an antiaircraft concealment scheme employed from June 1942 until the end of the war. It was a replacement for the earlier Measure 11 after feedback indicated that a darker shade of blue-gray was harder to see from the air. All vertical surfaces were painted in Navy Blue 5-N, with all decks in Deck Blue 20-B.

Measure 22: This was the most commonly applied US Navy camouflage scheme of the war, but was seldom used on carriers. It was a graded system providing good antisubmarine and antiaircraft concealment. Colors used included Haze Gray and Navy Blue; the Haze Gray was used on the upper hull, with the Navy Blue applied on the lower hull. Color separation was delineated on the main (hangar) deck level by a straight line running parallel to the horizon. White (5-U) was used in overhanging areas to reduce shadows. Flight decks were painted in Deck Blue.

Measure 32: This was a dazzle camouflage intended to provide antisubmarine protection by causing target angle confusion at close ranges. Several colors were authorized to be used in this scheme, including Pale Gray 5-P, Ocean Gray, Haze Gray, Navy Blue, and Dull Black 13. The flight deck remained in Deck Blue. This was regarded as the best antisubmarine scheme.

Measure 33: This was the refinement of other measures designed to give low-visibility antisubmarine protection. The colors used were Pale Gray, Ocean Gray, Haze Gray, and Navy Blue. White (5-U) was used under overhanging areas to alter the shadows.

Essex Class Camouflage:

Essex (CV-9): Commissioned in Ms 21. During her April 1944 refit, Ms 32/6-10d was applied. This dazzle scheme used only Pale Gray and Dull Black and was the only two-color dazzle scheme applied to any carrier. Deck numbers and dashed lines were in black and elevators were outlined in yellow. In 1945, the ship returned to Ms 21.

The deck markings of an *Independence* class carrier are clearly shown in this December 1943 view of *Belleau Wood*. The deck is in a dark blue stain with large numbers in black fore and aft. The flight deck stripes are in what appears to be white with yellow elevator edge markings.

Yorktown (CV-10): Commissioned in Ms 21. About March 1944, the ship was painted in Ms 33/10a. During her September 1944 refit, she returned to Ms 21.

Intrepid (CV-11): Commissioned in Ms 21. She received the dazzle Ms 32/3a in April 1944. This lasted only until December 1944, when the ship was painted in Ms 12. Deck numbers were in black with white dashed lines. Numbers and elevators were outlined in yellow.

Hornet (CV-12): Completed in Ms 33/3a, making her the first *Essex* to wear a dazzle scheme. The scheme was painted in Pale Gray, Haze Gray, and Navy Blue, making *Hornet* unique, as only she used the lighter Ms 33 colors. In September 1945, the ship received Ms 12. Deck numbers were in black with yellow dashed lines; the middle line was centered on the forward elevator instead of the usual practice of indicating the ship's centerline.

Franklin (CV-13): Commissioned in Ms 32/6a using Light Gray (5-L), Ocean Gray, and Dull Black. Curiously, in May 1944, her port side was repainted into design 3a using the same colors. She became the only carrier to wear two patterns simultaneously and her scheme was designated Ms 32/6a-3a. In January 1945, she was repainted in Ms 21. Deck numbers were in black with yellow outlines. Dashed lines on deck were in white with yellow elevator outlines and "X"s.

Ticonderoga (CV-14): Commissioned in Ms 33/10a with Light Gray, Ocean Gray, and Navy Blue. In 1945, she was painted in Ms 21 and her white deck dashed lines changed to black.

Randolph (CV-15): Commissioned in Ms 32/17a. This complex design required six colors: Pale Gray, Light Gray, Haze Gray, Ocean Gray, Navy Blue, and Dull Black. Her deck numbers were painted in white, making her the first wartime carrier with white deck numbers. In 1945, she was painted in Ms 21.

Lexington (CV-16): Commissioned in Ms 21. She was the only *Essex* never to receive a dazzle scheme; not surprisingly, she was nicknamed the "The Blue Ghost." In early 1945, *Lexington* was painted in Ms 12.

Bunker Hill (CV-17): Commissioned in Ms 21. She was painted in Ms 32/6a in January 1945, using Light Gray, Ocean Gray, and Dull Black. She and *Franklin* were the only *Essex* carriers to wear this scheme. In her January 1945 refit, she returned to Ms 21. Both outlines of deck numbers and deck dashed lines were painted in yellow.

Wasp (CV-18): Commissioned in Ms 21. Before she entered the Pacific, she was repainted in Ms 33/10a using Pale Gray, Haze Gray, and Navy Blue. *Wasp* returned to Ms 21 in 1945.

Hancock (CV-19): Commissioned in Ms 32/3a, using Light Gray, Ocean Gray, and Dull Black. She was the only long-hull *Essex* to use this scheme. *Hancock* was repainted in Ms 12 in June 1945.

Bennington (CV-20): Commissioned with the original version of Ms 32/17a. This used the same six colors as *Randolph*. In December 1944, she was repainted in a new simplified 17a design using only Haze Gray, Ocean Gray, and Navy Blue. In July 1945, she was repainted in Ms 21. Flight deck markings included black numbers and dashed lines (with no centerline marking) and no elevator outlines.

Bon Homme Richard (CV-31): Commissioned with the simplified Ms 32/17a identical to *Bennington*. She was repainted in Ms 12 in March 1945. Flight deck markings were the standard black numbers, white dashed lines, and elevators outlined with yellow "X"s.

Shangri-La (CV-38): Commissioned with Ms 33/10a using Light Gray, Ocean Gray, and Navy Blue. In 1945, she was repainted in Ms 21.

Independence Class Camouflage:

Independence (CVL-22): Commissioned in Ms 14. In June 1944, she was repainted in Ms 3_ /8a using Ocean Gray, Light Gray, and Navy Blue.

Princeton (CVL-23): Commissioned in Ms 14. She was repainted in Ms 33/7a in either January or May 1944 and was still wearing it when she was sunk. This measure used Haze Gray, Pale Gray, and Navy Blue.

Belleau Wood (CVL-24): Commissioned in Ms 21. Repainted in Ms 33/3d (a modified destroyer design) in August 1944. Colors used were Haze Gray, Pale Gray, and Navy Blue. Returned to Ms 21 during her January 1945 refit.

Cowpens (CVL-25): Commissioned in Ms 21. Repainted to Ms 33/7a in August 1944 using Dull Black for Navy Blue. The ship's final scheme was Ms 21, received in March 1945.

Monterey (CVL-26): Commissioned in Ms 22. In July 1944, she was painted in Ms 33/3d. *Monterey* returned to Ms 21 in January 1945.

Langley (CVL-27): Commissioned in Ms 21 and later painted in Ms 12. One of two *Independence* class carriers never to receive a dazzle scheme.

Cabot (CVL-28): Commissioned in Ms 21 and wore it her entire service life.

Bataan (CVL-29): Commissioned in Ms 3_ /8a with Pale Gray, Haze Gray, and Navy Blue.

San Jacinto (CVL-30): Commissioned in Ms 33/7a. She was repainted to Ms 21 after March 1945.

Bon Homme Richard in October 1945, just after the Japanese surrender. The ship is wearing a badly worn Measure 12 scheme. She has all late war modifications including the five starboard side sponsons and a modified bridge, and her SK-2 radar has been moved to a platform on the starboard side of the stack.

Independence in her original configuration with a bow-mounted single 5in/38 gun. Not visible is the second 5in gun fitted on the stern. Both were removed within weeks of commissioning. The ship is in a Measure 14 scheme.

A: USS *YORKTOWN* (CV-10), EARLY CONFIGURATION

These views show *Yorktown* as she appeared in the single-color Ms 21 scheme in summer 1943 before leaving the east coast for combat duty in the Pacific. This configuration is typical among early *Essex* class ships. The starboard side view shows the early radar fit consisting of an SK antenna on the forward part of the radar platform and an SC-2 antenna mounted on a platform on the starboard side of the stack. An SG radar is mounted on the topmast and there is a small radar platform for a second SG on the aft part of the stack. *Yorktown* carried ten 40mm quadruple mounts during this period; eight are visible here, including the four clustered forward and aft of the island, the bow mount, the single stern mount, and the two mounts on the starboard quarter at hangar deck level. The forward quadruple mount on the island was later removed to allow expansion of the flag bridge. Also visible are 23 20mm single mounts, most placed on the edge of the flight deck. The outrigger for the forward hangar deck catapult can also be seen in its stowed position. This was later removed. *Yorktown* was originally provided with five radio masts; later, only the two most forward masts were retained and whip antennae were placed aft. The overhead view shows the location of the two other 40mm quadruple mounts located near the single 5in/38 gun mounts forward and aft on the port side deck edge. A further 23 20mm single mounts are also visible, all but one located along the flight deck edge. This view also shows the facilities for handling aircraft, including the three elevators and a number of arresting wires on both the aft and forward areas of the flight deck.

B: USS *LEXINGTON* (CV-16), LATE WAR CONFIGURATION

These views show *Lexington* as she appeared in May 1945 after a refit that reflected all the late war weapons and electronics modifications made to *Essex* class ships. The ship appears in a two-tone Ms 12 scheme. The starboard side view shows the late war radar fit, consisting of an SM antenna on the forward part of the radar platform and the new SR antenna mounted on the aft portion of the radar platform in place of an SC-2. The SK-2 is mounted on a platform on the starboard side of the stack. By this period *Lexington* carried 17 40mm quadruple mounts; ten are visible here, including the three clustered forward and aft of the island (note the expansion of the flag bridge, requiring the removal of a quadruple mount), the bow mount, one of the two stern mounts, and five mounts on sponsons. The two on the starboard quarter have been placed in larger sponsons to improve their field of fire. The catapult has been removed from the forward hangar deck. *Lexington* retains only two radio masts, with four whip antennae fitted aft. The overhead view shows the location of four other 40mm quadruple mounts: two located near the single 5in/38 gun mounts forward and aft and two more located on platforms forward of the aft pair of 5in guns. The 20mm single mounts have been replaced with dual 20mm mounts and the overall number of gun positions has been reduced. *Lexington* was one of two ships to receive Army quadruple .50-cal. machine gun mounts; six are shown located on the 20mm gun platforms.

C: USS *TICONDEROGA* (CV-14), LONG-HULL *ESSEX* CLASS

These views show *Ticonderoga* as she appeared in May 1944 when commissioned. The ship appears in a dazzle Ms 33/10a scheme. Most of the late war configurations were incorporated into *Ticonderoga* when she was completed. The only difference between *Ticonderoga* and her short-hull sisters is the clipper bow that provided better sea-keeping qualities and allowed the fitting of a second 40mm quadruple mount on the bow with a better field of fire. The late war radar fit of an SM antenna on the forward part of the radar platform, with the large SK antenna mounted on the aft portion of the radar platform, is clearly shown. The SC-2 is mounted on a platform on the starboard side of the stack and an SG is fitted on the foremast. *Ticonderoga* was commissioned with 11 40mm quadruple mounts; nine are visible here, including the two mounts fitted on the forward port side of the hangar deck. The ship has the modified bridge. The overhead view shows two 40mm quadruple mounts on both the bow and the stern as well as the large number of 20mm single mounts grouped along the flight deck edge. The ship is fitted with two catapults and the arresting wires located on the forward portion of the flight deck are no longer evident. The flight deck stripe markings are in light gray; upon reaching the Pacific they were repainted in yellow.

D: USS *ESSEX*, AUGUST 1943

USS *Essex* was the lead ship of the largest class of fleet carriers ever built. With a well-balanced design offering speed, range, protection against air attack and a large air group, the *Essex* class was exactly what the US Navy needed as it brought the war ever closer to the Japanese Home Islands. Entering service on the last day of 1942, *Essex*'s combat career began in August 1943. She continued in service throughout the war, being damaged only once by kamikazes in November 1944. While not a perfect design, the *Essex* class proved very adaptable during the course of its Second World War service and was further modified after the war to serve into the jet age of US naval aviation. By virtue of its outstanding war service in the Pacific and its continued service into the Korean and Vietnam wars, the *Essex* class can be argued to have been the most successful carrier design in history.

E: THE *INDEPENDENCE* CLASS CARRIERS

This profile and plan of *Independence* shows her in her late war configuration. The small size of the island is clearly shown, as is the aircraft crane located forward of the island. The ship is in her late war Ms 3_/8a dazzle scheme. The primary modification following commissioning was the removal of the 5in mounts in favor of two quadruple 40mm mounts. In addition, the ship now fits nine dual 40mm mounts. The SK radar remains fitted between the four small smoke stacks, but the SC-2 has been replaced by an SM antenna on the radar platform. On the topmast is an SG radar and a YE homing beacon.

F: KAMIKAZES ATTACK *INTREPID*, NOVEMBER 25, 1944

The *Essex* class carrier most often struck by kamikazes was *Intrepid*. This scene shows the "Evil I" under attack on November 25 off Luzon. Two kamikazes crashed into the ship, resulting in a large fire on the hangar deck and the death of 65 crewmen. The fires were extinguished in less than two hours, but *Intrepid* left for repairs in the US the next day. The ship is pictured at the instant before the Japanese A6M "Zeke" (better known as the "Zero") hit the flight deck. The ship is in the Ms 32/3a scheme. Many late war modifications are evident, including the modified bridge, the SM and SK radars fitted on the radar platform, and 16 quadruple 40mm mounts, including two on the forward port side of the hangar deck and four located along the port edge of the flight deck.

G: *PRINCETON* IS BOMBED, OCTOBER 24, 1944

Princeton was the first and only US Navy light carrier lost during the war. This scene portrays the moment when the ship was struck by a single 550lb (250kg) bomb from a Japanese aircraft on October 24 during the battle for Leyte Gulf. The single bomb hit amidships and penetrated into the hangar bay, causing further explosions. Despite the efforts of the crew, almost six hours later the torpedo stowage area aft of the hangar bay ignited, causing a large explosion that devastated the ship and the light cruiser *Birmingham*, which was alongside providing fire-fighting support. *Princeton* was scuttled that evening after 114 of her crew had been killed and another 190 wounded. The ship is in an Ms 33/7a scheme and still retains an SC-2 radar on the forward part of the radar platform.

LEFT **After the war, the large numbers of *Essex* class carriers in service were superfluous to requirements and most were placed in reserve. This photograph of Puget Sound Navy Yard in Bremerton, Washington, in about 1948 shows *Essex*, *Ticonderoga*, *Yorktown*, *Lexington*, *Bunker Hill*, and in the distance *Bon Homme Richard*. All of these ships except *Bunker Hill* would eventually be modernized and returned to service.**

BELOW ***Independence* viewed from above in July 1943. The compact flight deck is clearly shown; combined with an even smaller hangar, this restricted the ship's air group to approximately 35 aircraft.**

INDEX

References to illustrations are shown in **bold**. Plates are shown with page and caption locators in brackets.

air groups 4–6
aircraft carriers:
    chronology 10–14
    doctrine 3
Amsterdam 39
atomic tests 39
Avenger bombers 5, 6, 38, 39, **41**

Bataan 12, **40**, 41–42, 45
Belleau Wood 10, 11, 40, 45
Bennington 13, 34, **35**, 45
Bon Homme Richard 13, 20, 34, 45, **45**, 47
Bunker Hill 10–11, 12, **14**, **22**, 24, **33**, 45, **47**

Cabot 11, 23, 39, 41, **42**, 45
camouflage 44–45
carrier task groups 3
Cleveland class cruisers 36
Combat Information Center 4
Corsair fighter 6, **19**
Cowpens 10, 11, **38**, 40, 45

Dauntless dive bombers 5, 6, 38, **41**
Dedalo 41

Enterprise 11, 12, 13
Essex 5, 10, 11, 12, 19–20, **19**, **D** (28–29, 47), **47**
Essex class fleet:
    action seen by 3
    air groups 4, 5, 6
    aircraft-handling facilities 17–18
    armament 16–17
    armor 15–16
    arresting gear 18
    assessment 35–36
    camouflage 44–45
    deck catapult 18
    deck park **18**

design and construction 15–16
    engines 16
    flight deck 15, 18, 44
    guns 7–8, **9**
    hulls 15
    main deck 15
    operational history 19–35
    origins 3, 14–15
    propulsion 16
    radar 7, 8, 9
    specifications 36
    wartime modifications 19

Fast Carrier Force 4, **4**, 11, 12, 14
Franklin 11, **11**, 12, **12**, 13, **21**, 22, 24, 44

General Motors 6
guns:
    5in/38 7, **7**, 16, 37
    Bofors 40mm 7–8, **8**, 16, **16**, **17**
    Oerlikon 20mm 8, 9, **9**, 17, 39

Hancock 13, 33–34, **34**, 44
Hellcat fighters **5**, 6, **6**, 12, **16**, **19**, 38, 39, **41**, **42**
Helldiver 6
Hiyo 40
Hornet **4**, **9**, 12, **13**, **18**, **20**, 21–22, 45

Independence 10, 11, **E** (30, 47), **38**, 39, 45, **46**, **47**
Independence class light carriers:
    action seen by 3
    air groups 4
    aircraft-handling facilities 38–39
    armament 37–38
    assessment 42–43
    camouflage 44, **44**, 45
    design and construction 37
    flight decks 44
    guns 7, 8, **8**
    losses **12**, 13
    operational histories 39–42
    origins 3, 36–37

radar 38
    specifications 43
Intrepid 11, **17**, 21, **F** (31, 47), 44, 45

kamikaze 4, 5, 6, **8**, 13, **13**, **15**, 40, 44, **F** (31, 47)
Korea 34

Langley **3**, 11, **37**, 41, 45
Lexington 10, 11, 12, **13**, **14**, 19, 23–24, **24**, **B** (26, 46), 45, **46**
logistics capability 4

Mitscher, Rear Admiral Mark 11
Monterey 11, 40, **42**, 45
Mushasi 13

Newark 42

Pearl Harbor 14, 21
Princeton 10, 11, **12**, 13, **G** (32, 47), 39–40, **41**, 45

radar 9–10, **11**
Randolph 13, 23, **23**
Roosevelt, President Franklin D. 36

San Jacinto 42, **43**, 45
Saratoga 10, 11
Shangri-La 13, 34–35, **35**, 45

Tallahassee 39
Ticonderoga **3**, **6**, **13**, 22–23, **22**, **C** (27, 46), 45

Ulithi Atoll **3**, **13**, **23**, **42**

Vietnam 20, 22, 23, 33, 34

Wasp 12, 13, 18, 24, 33, **33**, 45
Wildcat fighters 38

Yamato 13, 34
Yorktown 10, 11, 12, **13**, 14, 20, **A** (25, 46), 45, **47**